Praise for
Get Outta Your He~~au~~
and into your life

"*To my knowledge, it wasn't until Brené Brown and Gabrielle Bernstein that the millennials had strong female voices for their life challenges. I would put your book in that category - a book with longevity that will resonate with readers for years to come and be read over and over …*

… With its focus on personal choice, your book will give readers the nudge/kick/shove/push/validation/hope to grab their life and figure out how to survive and thrive despite what's going on around the world."

—Mary A. Metcalfe,
Author/Editor and Lifelong 'Work in Progress'

"*This book is empowering and a literary kaleidoscope of emotions, compelling the reader to look further into themselves and their surroundings for the answer that lies within. It is an amazing and immersive look at a young woman's journey into the wild, emerging with life lessons and heartfelt raw emotion that will leave all who encounter its pages a changed human for the better.*"

—Jeff Elamad, Health & Safety Officer and Father

"*I just finished the book and it's exactly what I needed to hear right now. Love the story and workbook combination - it's an amazing flow of work and play.*"

—Bay German, Mechanical Engineer, Husband, & Father

ISBN:

Printed Book: 978-1-7775470-0-4

E-Book: 978-1-7775470-1-1

GET OUTTA YOUR HEAD

and into your life

A GUIDE TO THRIVING IN OUR MODERN WORLD

KANDIS JAMES

Get Outta Your Head and into your life

Kandis James is the founder of *Live Your Dreams*, an online group coaching program designed to help others create a life they love to live each and every day. She's also an author, a business coach for James Wedmore's *Business by Design*, and an Applied Mindfulness and NLP Certified Life & Success Coach - but she prefers the title *Dream Life Strategist*

Kandis knows that the true meaning of life is happiness. And the only thing standing in anyone's way of achieving their dream life is their mind. She hopes to use her wealth of experience and knowledge to help millions of people get outta their head, and step into their best life.

DEDICATION

I'd like to dedicate this book to my great-grandmother, Nanna, and my grandmother, Mamie – two incredible women who have departed from this earth, but continue to guide me in their own unique ways.

And of course to my amazing parents, Rick and Sherry, whose unconditional love and support has never wavered as I continue to forge my way down unconventional paths in this wild ride we call life.

OH!

And I mustn't forget that random guy from Plenty of Fish (POF. com) I went on a date with way back when. I can't remember his name – but he changed the trajectory of my life forever. Wherever you are, dude, thank you!

CONTENTS

AUTHOR'S NOTE

'M WHITE, I'M blonde, and I was born and raised in a safe suburban city in Canada.

So just right there I understand I haven't been faced with many of the same difficulties as some of you who are reading this book.

My dad worked 60+ hours per week as a used car salesman while my mom stayed home to raise us kids. I grew up in a middle class neighborhood, I was surrounded by my cousins growing up, my parents are still together, and I have a great relationship with them.

I almost died when I was three from an extremely rare and extremely deadly virus.

I am also part of the 17 per cent official statistics of women who have been raped or who have experienced attempted rape in North

America. (I've experienced both.) And of course, we all know that the unreported cases would greatly increase that number.

I have been in many relationships where I was treated terribly, cheated on, lied to, even hit.

I have also had amazing relationships that showed me what true love really can look like.

Each and every one of us has our unique story. And it's not about who has more trauma, more difficulties, or more struggles. The message I bring to you is that no matter what is going on in your external reality, you can *choose* how you show up to it each and every day. You can *choose* what it means for you and for your future. For some, choosing positivity and light will be more difficult. For others it will be easier. But the ease with which we can venture forward with joy and peace of mind doesn't necessarily correlate with what is happening in our external world.

The ease with which we float through life is based upon our ability to cultivate strength and happiness within. It is based on our ability to strengthen our mind to the point where no matter what is going on around us, we can remain detached and main-

The ease with which we float through life is based upon our ability to cultivate strength and happiness within.

tain a sense of calm. And don't take this to mean that we don't care about what is happening. That's not it at all. Rather, it means you achieve a level of stability of mind by which your happiness is cultivated within, unable to be destroyed by external events or things you cannot control. And in fact, as you dive into your mindfulness journey you might even notice that you find yourself having *more intense* feelings and connections to other humans, animals, causes, and situations. Because the more you follow this path, the more you open yourself up to, and learn from, the universe.

It's always important to have these things in your awareness. And as we will discuss in the coming pages, it's also important that you don't *attach* to them. I am now able (most of the time) to acknowledge, understand, and attempt to heal the pain and turmoil that our world is in right now, the pain I experience personally, and the pain my loved ones experience, while I maintain my positive personal energy.

And I hope the same for you.

I spread my message and my own learnings on these pages with the hope that I can play some small role in making your days a little brighter, a little more beautiful.

Much love, peace, and laughter,

Kandis ♥

CHAPTER 1

Creating Your Reality

IT'S TRULY AMAZING how one realization – one shift within the mind – can completely change someone's life, which in this case was mine. The morning after my life-changing realization inspired by a man whose name I now can't remember, I woke up with a newfound pep in my step.

I was going to Thailand!

I was going to travel the world!

I was going to start living my dreams, and it felt as real as real could be. It was no longer a matter of *if* I would go, it was simply a matter of *when*.

And this time, when my current reality smacked me in the face (i.e., my expensive condo rent, credit card debt, monthly payments, 'can't miss' family events, and all the other things that had long been the reasons for my not moving forward), I didn't even flinch. Yesterday, all these things were reasons for why I wasn't able to travel. Today, they were simply obstacles that needed to be acknowledged, accepted, and then removed. And the cool thing?

I knew then, as I know even more deeply now, that I am not only 100% responsible for making choices in my life that lead me to the life I love ... but also that I am the *only* one who is capable of taking myself there.

And so, I was off to the races.

I arrived at work and immediately set my computer desktop to the image of Thailand with 'Wake Up to What You Choose' written across it. And then that day, and every day for the next several weeks, I spent every free moment I could find at the office (and when I got home), researching where I wanted to go, how much it would cost, and what travel equipment I would need to make this happen. The more I researched Thailand, Laos, Cambodia, Vietnam, and the rest of Southeast Asia, the more focused I became on achieving my goal and the more I knew without a doubt, all through my body, that this trip was finally going to be a reality.

And from that fateful day, until I set foot on an airplane fourteen months later, I worked my freakin' butt off to create that reality!

You see, when I tell you that you can create your reality, it's not as simple as waving a magic wand, or rubbing a genie lamp and making a wish – although that would be pretty freakin' rad! Instead, creating the life you desire takes focused attention, clarity, creativity and dedication.

Creating the life you desire takes focused attention, clarity, creativity and dedication.

Outwardly, I had done 'all the things'. I'd gone to school, got the job, got the beautiful condo, blah blah blah … and yet I couldn't help but wonder … where do my dreams, goals, and desires fit into this? Where is the fun, excitement, and adventure in this life? Where is the wonder, awe, and inspiration that I know this world has to offer?

Shouldn't I be happier than this?

I knew I was meant for more than what I was experiencing. But what did 'more' mean, exactly? And how was I supposed to get there?

I would often find myself tired and burnt out, daydreaming about traveling to far-off lands – specifically Thailand – and wondered what it would be like to set off one day to discover them. To create a new life somewhere – a life full of new cultures, new people, new foods, new landscapes. A life full of adventure and possibility. A life I could create and live on my own terms.

And then the phone would ring, or my boss would yell something out to me, or I'd look at my measly bank account that had been dwindling from all my fashion shopping, and I'd be thrown back into 'reality'. Everything I'd dreamt about was far away once again, and it all seemed just about as possible as winning the lottery one day.

"Who am I kidding?" I would say to myself. "I have bills to pay, responsibilities to take care of. These dreams are just dreams. Possible for others, but not for me. Not now. Besides, my life isn't that bad is it? Many people would love to have my life just as it is."

And so I would once again push the dreams out of my mind, and get back to 'real life'.

And then something happened that would change the trajectory of my life forever: I met a guy off an Internet dating site.

This was back in 2010 when Internet dating was fresh, and we were all on POF.com

He and I chatted briefly online and decided to meet up. He came one cool autumn evening to pick me up at my condo building and we walked to grab a drink at a nearby pub in Liberty Village – the Brazen Head. We sat in the dimly lit room not far from the bustle of the bar, and chatted as we sipped our beer. First date chatter of course … getting to know one another. And he began telling me stories of his backpacking trips all over the world. It was when he got to the part about Southeast Asia that his stories especially caught my attention: the people he met, the adventures he went on, the food he ate, and the cultures he experienced. If my jaw wasn't hitting the floor, it might as well have been. I was listening in utter awe, hanging on every word.

"I wish I could do that," I finally muttered.

"Why can't you?" he asked.

"Because I've got a job, and bills to pay. I've got a life here," I replied.

"So it's not that you can't, it's that you aren't making it a priority," he said casually.

I shrugged my shoulders and the topic changed. We stayed for a couple more hours before walking back to my condo where we hugged goodbye and went our separate ways. The conversation had been interesting, but there was no spark, no *'je ne sais quoi'* and so we never texted, called, or saw each other again. But I do deeply wish that now I could remember his name. Because I would so love to find him and tell him what a profound effect that evening had on me. Those fourteen words he so casually spoke that evening would change my life forever.

You see, when I got up to my apartment that night, I couldn't stop thinking about what he'd said: *It's not that I couldn't travel, it's that I wasn't making it a priority.*

And it was then that a thought came over me.

I heard a voice in my head that said, "You wake up to what you choose.

I suddenly had goosebumps all over my body. I repeated it to myself. "You wake up to what you choose."

My subconscious mind had heard this man's message loud and clear. If I want something in life, it's up to me to make it happen. It was suddenly so clear to me. I was twenty-six years old. I could *choose* to keep making excuses and continue to live a life that was not what I'd dreamed of, yet was familiar and comfortable. Or, I could *choose* to take action, step out of my comfort zone, and actually start living the life I dreamed of every single day.

Why was I spending my days living here, and dreaming of elsewhere when I could just LIVE THOSE DREAMS instead?

To me, 'wake up to what you choose' was so powerful because it was a realization that every morning when I wake up, I am waking up to my own reality that I created through the culmination of all the choices I made leading up to that moment. And so the only way to change the reality to which I wake up each morning, is by making different choices the day before. And thus, we wake up to what we choose.

Every. Single. Day.

And so I needed to decide: what was I going to choose for myself moving forward?

If I choose to spend four hundred dollars on designer jeans, then I wake up the next day with four hundred dollars less in my savings account and feelings of anxiety over paying my rent. If I choose to drink a bunch of alcohol at the bar one night, then I wake up the next day with a hangover. If I choose to spend money on expensive rent and parties, then I wake up the next day without enough money to pay for a flight or book a trip to where I want to go.

These were the things I had been making a priority in my life. Clothing, parties, a fancy apartment – but not anymore.

I opened up my laptop and found an image of Thailand – the place I wanted to go most in the world. I put the words "Wake Up to What You Choose" over the image and set it as my desktop wallpaper. Then I emailed the image to my work email address so I could do the same thing when I arrived at the office the next morning.

Original graphic that I created. Check out those design skills!

I went to bed with a sense of excitement. I was no longer going to worry about what I was 'supposed to do'. Nor would I simply let life happen to me. Going to Thailand wasn't going to solve my 'problem' of what business to start, or what exactly to do with my life ... but I knew that I needed to experience something new. And so I was going to stop making excuses and finally just do it! I could feel it in my bones that my life was about to shift. Because in that moment, I understood in a deeply profound way that I, and I alone, am responsible for the creation of my life.

I, and I alone, am responsible for the creation of my life.

And that *every* choice I make will either take me closer to or farther away from where I truly want to go, and who I truly want to be in this life. In that moment, I understood that I am 100% responsible for creating the life I'd been dreaming of.

I lay in bed that night excited to begin making choices that only brought me closer to those dreams.

And as it turns out ... this realization was just the seedling of a much greater message that the universe was unfolding in front of me.

point, I was using cocaine every single day, and I was taking ecstasy tablets before joining friends for a casual barbecue on a Sunday afternoon.

As I said – outwardly, I 'had it all'. Inwardly, I was empty.

I felt like I was becoming a shell of myself. Like I had to discard the person I truly was in order to be the person who was able to keep up with the Joneses. The designer clothing that I would wear only one time in the same city was racking up the debt on my credit cards at a rapid pace. And then to make sure I looked good in the designer clothes I kept buying, I was taking illegal diet pills on the daily. There was a time when my routine consisted of coming home from work around 5:30 p.m., grabbing a pickle and a vodka and Diet Coke for my dinner, before a friend or two would come round to start in on the cocaine for the rest of the evening, barely pulling it together for work the next morning, and then doing it all again. I won't even get started on what went on over the weekends. But let me tell you, combining diet pills, drugs, alcohol, and late nights on the regular makes for one irritable, exhausted, and wildly unhealthy gal. In fact, looking back, I'm not sure how my heart kept up with all the destruction.

But then on top of it all – or perhaps the fuel of it all – I had dreams and desires that reached beyond the walls of the boxed in world I was living in. I wanted to shed those fancy clothes for flip-flops and a backpack to travel the world. I wanted to start my own business, although I had no idea what specifically I would do. I just knew that I wanted to make a difference in people's lives. And I wanted to be able to live my life the way I wanted, not the way I was being told to live by society, the government, my parents, etc.

… I felt stuck.

PREFACE

"Wake Up to What You Choose"

I WAS IN MY early twenties and doing everything I thought I was supposed to do. I had finished college, and I'd moved to the 'big city' of Toronto. I was working a job that paid good money. I was invited to all the coolest parties, and I wore designer clothes to each of them. People thought I had such a cool life. In fact, I thought I had a cool life too – at first.

Outwardly, it appeared I 'had it all'. The clothes, the parties, the condo, the men, the admirers. I could skip the lines at the hottest nightclubs, and I got free passes and invitations to every party including Fashion Week and the Toronto International Film Festival (TIFF). I even had my picture taken for the local 'Who's Who' pages once or twice.

What a lot of people didn't see, however, was that the parties were fuelled by way too many drugs and far too much alcohol. At one

Throw in a bit of intuition, perseverance, resilience, adaptability, and sheer hard work, and you're just about there! (Don't worry, we'll go over all of this in more detail later in the book.)

As I said, I was off to the races.

Making Choices to Move Closer to My Goal

I calculated the approximate cost of what a 3–4 month backpacking trip would cost and started making choices that would move me closer to my goal. The first of those choices was finding a way to decrease my living expenses.

I gave up my expensive shoebox-sized condo and put a deposit on a cheap four-bedroom house at the cross-sections of Toronto's Little Italy, Little Portugal, and Little Korea. (Talk about amazing food selections nearby!) Next, I put up a Craigslist ad to find three roommates and started interviewing right away. Some days, I think I could write a book just about *that* experience alone!

But the interview that stuck out to me the most was meeting a guy I later nicknamed 'The Beer Drinking Thief'. This guy showed up in a stained T-shirt, stinking of stale beer, telling me that his hobbies involved drinking beer and watching TV, and then proceeded to tell me a story about how he stole five hundred dollars worth of stuff from his previous roommate. I looked around for the hidden cameras, but nobody popped out asking me to sign a TV release form, so as far as I know, this guy just legitimately thought this would be a great story to help him find a roommate. He did score a couple points for honesty though, I must say.

Thankfully, life is all about balance. I was getting very tired of the interview process by the time Alix came to meet me inside Toronto's oldest pub for a pint, and we ended up ordering a second round of drinks after we found ourselves laughing and talking effortlessly together for an hour. She told me she'd take the apartment right then and there – without having seen the place in person. And now, ten years later, we're still very close friends, having visited each other in multiple cities around the world.

Eventually, I found all three roommates: Alix, Tim, and Tom. I also found a part-time job as a receptionist at a chiropractic clinic three evenings a week and full-day Saturdays. On top of that I was taking every random job someone offered me. I sold glowing toys at the Canadian National Exhibition, I cleaned student housing (ew!), and did odd jobs for family and friends.

I was so freakin' busy making money every way I could imagine that it was truly a whirlwind of a year.

But all the tired nights and early mornings paid off. In just that one year, I saved more than enough for my trip. Things were really happening now! I remember my mom taking me shopping at this crowded little outdoors/adventure shop downtown. She and my dad had decided to buy my backpack for me as a Christmas gift, and there we were, a pile of bags in front of me, trying to find the right size, the right color, the right fit. Gosh, I was excited. Just thinking back on that now, I can't help but beam a smile across my face almost the same size as the one I wore that night. I was grinning from ear to ear, practically bouncing with excited energy. I knew that my life was shifting. Things were happening. I was not just opening a new chapter, but a whole damn new book.

Pushing Past My Comfort Zone

I had my entire trip planned out. I was going to start in Europe to see Alix, who had since moved back to Europe for a job, followed by a 65-day tour to Thailand, Laos and Cambodia. After that, I would take a flight to Perth to meet a friend for seven days, before heading to Melbourne where I planned to stay for a year. I had received a working holiday visa for Australia, and my 3–4 month trip was now looking like it would be a year instead.

My parents took me to the airport in May of 2011. They stayed with me and had some food at the airport Swiss Chalet while I waited for my flight. Leaving them was bittersweet. I had no idea when I'd be home. It was incredibly exciting, terrifying, and sad all in one. I simultaneously wanted to jump up and down with excitement and then break down and cry, burying myself into my parents' arms. Since then, I realize that's what it often feels like when you're stepping so far outside your comfort zone. That mix of excitement and fear. Of 'heck ya!' and 'OH SHIT!' all at once. I recognize it now so easily because I consistently do what I can to push past my comfort zone. Because let me tell you – that is where all of life's spectacular things happen. And then I hugged my parents for the last time and walked towards airport security. We all had tears in our eyes as I waved and mouthed one last 'I LOVE YOU!' and walked through the gates.

A New Chapter Begins

When I touched down at Charles de Gaulle airport in Paris, Alix was waiting for me with a huge sign to welcome my arrival. We found the car and went directly to her brother's apartment, which he'd graciously offered us as he and his wife were headed on their honeymoon later that day. It was about 7:00 a.m. on a beautiful, sunny, spring morning in the center of Paris. As we walked from where we parked the car, I remember seeing hundreds of locals bustling about, and I swear at least half of them were carrying a baguette. Alix and I laughed at my strange tourist observation of her home city. When we arrived at her brother's place, we used one of those old elevators where you have to pull iron gates closed and lock them in place before pushing the button for your floor. Her brother greeted us at the door to his apartment and my cheeks blushed red as I fumbled my words, calling upon my ill-remembered high school French. He invited us in for breakfast, and we sat at the table ripping apart our baguettes and enjoying them with jam and coffee.

The window in the living room opened outward, allowing me to lean out over the streets of Paris. Tired from the flight, full from the breakfast, and wildly excited about what lay ahead, I took in a deep breath, noticing the new smells, listening to the sounds of the streets below, and soaking in the sights of the old, Parisian buildings. I'd been to Paris twice before – briefly – but this time it was different. This time I was there with a local, living in a downtown apartment for two weeks. *And* … it was the stepping-stone to my grand adventure. The butterflies of excitement were welling up inside me. My journey had truly begun. And in just a couple of weeks I would be in Thailand. My wildest dreams were coming true!

Entering the Land of Smiles

I still remember getting struck by the smell and feel of Bangkok as I walked from the freezing cold air-conditioned interior of Suvarnabhumi Airport to the outdoors – the hot, humid air so thick it was almost as though I could feel myself walking through it. And it was accompanied by a smell. Not a bad smell. But a smell that anyone who has ever flown into Bangkok knows as the smell of Bangkok. Thick and distinct, it's a smell I eventually associated with being home.

Confused, exhausted, overwhelmed, and excited all in one, I managed to get a taxi to my guesthouse, The Wild Orchid. As we drove down the highway and made our way to the backpacker's hub known as Khao San Road, I marveled at sights that were entirely new to me. It was a major city. And yet, it was like nothing I'd ever seen. Tall apartment buildings, filthy on the outside, laundry on a string hanging from each balcony, all standing next to the most modern, brilliant buildings I'd ever seen. It appeared that esthetics were important, but even more so, practicality and functionality.

The taxi came to its final stop, and as I opened the door I was hit again with vibrant smells, this time of food stalls that lined the street, which were accompanied by the sound of local shopkeepers trying to entice wandering tourists inside. The guesthouse had a grand, open entrance, full of heavy teak furniture that at the time looked unique and exotic and would eventually become so normal I most often forgot to appreciate its beauty.

I thanked the driver and checked into my room. It was a basic room that looked like the walls could use a good scrubbing with soap and water, but the sheets were crisp and clean and I threw my backpack down onto the queen-sized bed. I had to pee so badly, and suddenly I was hit with the realization that there was no bathroom in my room! I looked around and saw the door I'd come in, and the sliding door to the balcony. But where was the bathroom?

Not knowing what else to do, I slid open the door to the balcony, and to my surprise, there was the door to my private bathroom. Yes, accessed by the balcony. And the 'air holes' in the side of the walls opened the bathroom up to the sounds and smells of the busy streets below.

I didn't know it then, but that was the first of *many* interesting bathroom experiences in Asia.

An Adventure into the Unknown

After figuring out how to use the now beloved 'bum gun', I changed into something more appropriate for the thick, wet air and left the hotel to find some of that authentic Thai food I'd been drooling over in my mind since I first wrote 'You Wake Up To What You Choose' on an image of Thailand over a year before.

It had been about eighteen months since that night at the Brazen Head. In eighteen months, my life had completely flipped around. I'd quit the job that left me feeling unfulfilled. I'd given up my apartment, sold most of my belongings, and put whatever was left in a box in my parents' basement.

At the age of twenty-seven, most of my friends back home were diving into their careers, getting married, and buying houses.

And here I was arriving in Thailand, just me and my backpack - no longer a dream, it had become my reality.

The joy in my heart center swelled up.

I felt pride for getting myself there. I felt excitement for what lay ahead. And I couldn't help thinking to myself, *Holy shit, is this for real?*

Writing this now, I find myself tearing up with emotion. As I look back on myself and who I was in that moment, I smile. That was the first time in my life I had taken such a giant leap outside

I felt like I was truly experiencing life just as it was. Just as it is.

my comfort zone. It was the first time in my life I threw away the 'should do's, the 'should have's, and the 'should be's and finally said yes to my heart – and yes to myself. And here I was in Thailand. I was so excited. And also completely unaware of the true power of the leap I had taken and the effect it would have on my life.

For the first time, I felt like I was truly experiencing life just as it was. Just as it is. No job to worry about, no commitments to adhere to. I had jumped in with both feet, accepting an adventure into the unknown.

I sat down at a restaurant near the guesthouse and ordered my first of many Thai curries and a large bottle of Chang Beer.

The cold beer felt perfect as it hit my lips, bringing a smile of pure joy to my face for the millionth time that day.

In that moment, this particular meal meant so much more to me than new flavors and sustenance. It meant more than trying an exotic dish in a new country. In that moment, this meal represented all the hours I'd put in working to save money. It represented the belongings I'd sold, the planning I'd done, and the goodbyes I had said that cumulatively brought me to Thailand in that moment.

This basic Thai meal represented a dream come true.

And so when that meal arrived on my table, I almost cried. I almost cried because I was so proud of myself for finally doing something that I'd dreamt of for so long.

And little did I know then, it also represented the beginning of a five-and-a-half-year love affair with a country and its people.

The Theories Behind Chapter 1

"You wake up to what you choose."

The thought popped into my mind that fateful day, and everything became so clear to me in that moment.

Each and every day you make a cascade of choices.

Most of us wake up each morning and choose to brush our teeth. Then we choose to have a shower, and we choose to go to work. We might say we "have to" go to work, but in reality, nobody is holding a gun to our head. Most of us choose to go to work because we want the paycheck, right? We want to be able to pay for food, shelter, etc. So we choose to go to work. We choose to eat breakfast first (or not) and we choose whether we drive, walk, or take transit.

And each and every one of these choices has a consequence. Some immediate, and some farther down the road.

Here are a few examples:

CHOICE	CONSEQUENCE
Hit the snooze button.	Late for work or rushed getting ready.
Don't eat breakfast.	Hungry before lunch break.
Eat McDonald's for lunch.	Have a stomachache.
Drink too many martinis.	Deal with a hangover.
Eat a full cheesecake every day.	Gain 10 pounds in a month.
Do crunches every day.	Have a 6-pack next year.
Eat well AND do crunches every day.	Have a 6-pack in 6 months.

Spend all my money on designer clothes.	Have no money for travelling.
Eat the whole chocolate bar now.	Don't have any chocolate later.
Grab a girl's butt on the street.	Get punched in the face.

I hope you see where I'm going with this?

Every time we choose to do something, we are not only saying yes to that particular action, but we're saying yes to the consequences or the automatic events that go with it!

So essentially … each day when we wake up, we're waking up to the choices that we made the day(s) before.

It seems so simple, and yet the majority of people in this world are not taking responsibility for their life. They're not taking responsibility for the choices they've made that got them to where they are. And every day, many people are making choices that will bring them further from where they really want to be in life.

I see it all the time. People complain about how much they hate their job, but then for 10 years, they get up five days a week and keep going back without ever looking for a new one. They say they can't afford to travel, but then drop $2,000 every time Apple releases the latest iPhone. They tell you how badly they want to lose weight as they're placing an order for the extra-large super king-size combo with extra fries.

When I first coined the term 'wake up to what you choose', it meant that I was the *only person* who had control over my life. That if I want something in life, I've got to take 100% responsibility in making whatever that is happen. That I had to take responsibility for not just every direct choice that I make, but for each one of the consequences, or 'automatic events', that go along with those. It was an understanding that saying yes to three large slices of chocolate cake one time won't have great implications (except for, perhaps, a stomachache) ... but if I continue to say yes to three slices of chocolate cake on a daily basis, I'm going to gain weight. Perhaps even, it could lead to diabetes.

See, you can dream all you want. You can wish for things to be different. But until you put one foot in front of the other and take action each and every day *toward those dreams,* then guess what? Things will stay exactly the same. And for some, they'll even continue to get worse.

And so I thought to my self, "Okay Kandis, you want to travel? You want to change up your life? Then what are you waiting for? Your NEXT life?"

Learning to Take Responsibility

When I had this realization, it had already been about five years since I'd been introduced to the concept of mindfulness, although that's not what I knew it as then.

In 2005, I had just moved to Toronto and was going to George Brown College for a certificate program in Image Consulting. I was learning how to help others achieve their utmost potential through appearance, behavior and communication skills. It was in that class that my freakin' amazing teacher and program founder, Karen Brunger, introduced me to the book *The Power of Now* by Eckhart Tolle.

At that time, I was working full-time at an upscale private medical clinic, part-time as a cigarette girl at concerts dressed in cowboy boots and a hat and snorting cocaine before class to keep up with my insane schedule and let's face it, my drug problem. The first time I read the book, I was more than intrigued, but also incredibly confused. I highlighted parts of the book that really stood out to me, and despite not understanding approximately 70–80% of the book, I began implementing what I did understand. It was the first time I'd heard of the concept:

> *"We are not our mind, and neither is our brain. We have the ability to 'watch the thinker' and choose to take responsibility, and respond instead of react."*

> —Eckhart Tolle, *The Power of Now*

So, I started changing small things, like how I responded to a traffic jam. Where I used to get emotionally upset and angry about a traffic jam, I now did my best to simply let it be, and not get caught up in things I couldn't change. It was a bit of a struggle at first, my intention fighting against my natural instinct, but like all things it got easier over time.

And it wasn't until that date with the man whose name I don't know that I unlocked something within me. I realized these practices expanded much further than how I reacted to a traffic jam. That through these practices I understood that I had a CHOICE every day, every moment. By choosing how to *It is only this moment that we ever truly have.* respond in each moment of each day, I could take control of the trajectory of my life. Because it is only *this moment* that we ever truly have. The past is gone, and the future is in our imagination until it becomes the present moment. And instead of allowing life to happen *to me*, I could *choose to create it* in every single moment.

Will You Choose to be a Victim of Life? Or the Creator?

As Eckhart Tolle says in *The Power of Now*, there is a difference between your life, and your life situation.

Your life situation is your job, your spouse (or lack thereof), your house, your car, your health, your family, their health, the family drama. It's the stock market, it's politics, and it's global warming. It's how you treat others and how they treat you.

Now, I'll invite you to pause for a moment.

Relax your shoulders. Relax your jaw, your eyebrows, your forehead. Close your eyes and take in a deep breath.

Are you doing it?

Allow that breath to fill your chest, your lungs, and then release it. Let it go. *This* is life.

Can you smell anything? Hear anything? Feel anything? *This* is life.

Take another deep breath, and this time curl up the outer corners of your mouth as you do so, creating a very gentle smile. And then release that breath, the corners of your mouth still turned up.

This is life. And it's *never* to be confused with or mistaken for your life situation.

Being able to separate your life from your life situation is a vital part of not only creating success during your lifetime, but also the ability to do it from a place of freedom, possibility, and joy instead of stress, fear, and restraint. And the more adept you become at being able to quickly analyze which is which as it's happening, the easier it will become to take a pause, and choose the best course of action in that moment.

There are Three Sides to Every Story

When it comes to creating your own reality, it's not just about what you consciously choose to create – although that is a big part of it. But it's important to realize that there is also a lot of stuff going on subconsciously, which means you're creating new realities each and every moment without even thinking about it.

The complexity of the human brain and self-aware mind is the uniqueness that sets us apart from other animals. SUPER RAD! Also, super complicated.

I liken it to riding a horse. I've ridden a horse three times that I can remember. All three of those times, the horse and I started out just taking a slow, pleasant wander from the yard where someone had helped me on, only to find a few minutes later the horse is galloping through a field at full speed, almost taking off my head on low-hanging tree branches while I hang on for dear life, screaming OMG!! HOLY SHIT! WTF!

If you don't learn how to command that horse and take control of the reins, it doesn't matter where *you* want to go. That horse will take you wherever *it* wants to go, and there won't be anything you can do about that.

Our mind has the same power.

When you find yourself caught in a loop of worry, stress, anxiety, self-deprecation, or any other negative spiral of thought, it is exactly like this horse situation. It means you've let go of the reins, and your mind is running wild. It's going places you likely don't want to go, creating realities you probably don't want to live in.

And so, when I say there are three sides to every story, it's because when an event happens in our life situation, an unattended mind will begin to immediately create some stories about the events that just took place.

We receive information about the outside world through our five senses. The information is then sent to the main command station (aka the brain) and then we interpret it based on, well, based on a lot of things. But, the brain sits inside a dark room, not physically connected to anything it sees, hears, feels, smells, or tastes.

> *The brain sits inside a dark room, not physically connected to anything it sees, hears, feels, smells, or tastes.*

One of the major things we base interpretations on is our past experience. You see, the brain's job is to take in as much information as possible at all times, and analyze it as quickly as possible so that it can always be ready to alert us to any danger.

Here's an interesting fact:

The brain receives approximately 11 million pieces of information per second. And it's believed that we can be consciously aware of up to just 40 pieces of that information at any given time.

Wild, right?

For example, I'm currently sitting in my apartment. I'm writing this book, and simultaneously I'm consciously aware of the candles flickering beside me, the traffic noises coming from outside the window, the music playing from my Bluetooth speaker in the corner, and my two cats playing some weird game together in the other room. I'm also vaguely aware of the feeling of my hands on the keyboard/blanket, and the fact that my butt is starting to get pins and needles from sitting in one position for too long. And of course, I am looking at my iPad where I'm typing this, and in my peripheral vision I can see the window, walls, bookshelf, lamp, etc.

And at the same time, my unconscious or subconscious mind is aware of so much more. And it's constantly checking the information it's receiving against what it already knows from past experience, so that it can ensure that I'm safe. So now imagine that all of a sudden, I'm aware of a strange noise. I'm yanked out of my focused writing state, I sit up straight, thinking, "What was that?" and I shush everyone and everything around as I attempt to listen closer.

Why am I doing this?

Because while I was sitting there writing, my brain was constantly scanning all ~11 million pieces of stimulus it was receiving and checking it against what it believes is 'normal' in this situation, based on its past experience. And that random noise it heard didn't fit. So it sent a signal that basically said, "Alert! I don't recognize that noise! I have nothing to base it on. You might be in danger!" And that's enough to fire up the ol' fight or flight stress response system inside the body to physically make me more alert.

And then once I realize that it was just the cat pushing things off the shelf (as he likes to do), then my system relaxes, and I can continue to focus on typing these words, or whatever it was I was doing before my brain sent this alert.

Perhaps you've noticed that when you're staying at someone else's house, or you've just moved into a new place, that there are often times when 'weird sounds' can keep you up at night. That's because your brain doesn't recognize them. It doesn't know what a 'normal' noise is for this new location, and thus it remains on high alert. Once you spend more time in that place, the brain begins to recognize those 'weird' noises as regular occurrences that bring no danger, and it labels them as 'normal' for that situation. Once it's no longer on high alert for each noise, the brain can rest, and you can sleep!

A perfect example of this is when I used to live in downtown Toronto. There were 24-hour streetcars, buses, and regular traffic just below my window all night every night. For the first week after I moved in, I had difficulty sleeping. I was waking up each time the streetcar rang its bell or the cars at the traffic light honked their horns. But soon enough I slept perfectly soundly and was only reminded about how much noise there really was when I would have a guest stay over and they found it difficult to sleep because their own brain hadn't yet classified these noises as 'normal'.

The Fight/Flight/Freeze Response (The Basics)

Throughout the duration of this book (as you may have already noticed) I'll be mentioning the fight/flight/freeze response frequently. And that's because it's essentially at the very core of our human existence. It's activated by one of the earliest parts of the human brain, and it's also the part of our brain that keeps us out of danger's way. I'll go over this in more detail later, but the important thing you need to know right now is that it's this fight/flight/freeze response (let's call it the FFF response) that allows us to run for long distances at high speeds when we're outrunning danger or gives us 'superhuman' strength in an emergency. It's the reason that you hear stories about near death experiences where people say, *'I have no idea how I did what I did to get away … but suddenly there I was!* And it's the same response that had my mother sitting in her pajamas, bare feet in the snow, drying off our dog Buddy after she pulled him from the pool where he'd fallen through the ice. In the moment of a dearly beloved being in a situation where he could die, the cold didn't matter to my mother at all, and she acted from pure instinct to get out there and do what it took to get the dog out of the freezing water.

That's what the FFF response looks like on the outside.

On the inside, the simplified explanation is that your body releases a large dose of cortisol (the 'stress hormone') and adrenaline into your system. Also during this state, your brain shuts down specific areas of the brain that aren't necessary to your survival in that moment so that it can send more energy to other areas that are deemed important to escape the danger. This is why some people experience 'superhuman strength' in life or death situations.

The point of all this being …

Your brain is constantly trying to keep you safe. That's its job.

It is constantly comparing your current situation to situations it has known in the past, so that it can decide if what's happening *now*, is something that could put you in danger. And because the brain has such an intense job, and literally works 24/7; it's a wildly efficient little machine that is constantly trying to do things while expending as little energy as possible.

And it's this comparison that our brain makes to past experiences that is the main reason why we each experience everything in life just a little (or a lot) differently.

And that's why I said there are three sides to every story:

1. My side

2. Your side

3. The truth

Three sides of course, if it's just you and I involved. If my whole family of 35 people were involved (imagine a holiday dinner), then there become 36 sides to every story. Each one of those 35 people will have a slightly different version or perception of how that dinner unfolded. And then of course, there will be the truth – the *actual* events, words, and actions that transpired – equaling 36 separate versions or perceptions of that evening.

For example, around 2006 I was driving my sister and our cousin home from Chicago to Toronto. We'd been down to the US for my grandfather's funeral, and we left Chicago at 8 p.m. to make the nine- hour drive home to be back in time for work the next day. When we left it was already dark. My cousin had recently been in a very bad car accident where she had to be extracted from the car by firefighters. The whole drive (until she finally fell asleep in the back seat) she was gripping the seats, letting out muffled yelps when I would switch lanes or tap on the brakes. She was just generally terrified.

Then there was my sister. She's never felt comfortable driving. Especially at night. Especially on roads that she doesn't know. Especially in the US. And especially when it's raining (which it started to do at one point). To top it off, she needs glasses to see any type of distance at all. She kept saying to me in a voice wavering with nervousness, "I think we should pull over. I can't see anything!" to which I would reply, "Well then it's a good thing I'm the one driving!"

I was tired, of course, especially with the anxiety from the passengers. But aside from that, I was perfectly confident and comfortable with the drive.

Same car. Same situation. Three wildly different responses.

And if I were to get those two together right now and have them both tell their version of the story, you'd see that their perception of events had variations from my own, especially since the whole situation was almost 15 years ago. Perhaps they don't remember the event. Or, perhaps they remember each response in a completely different way than I do. And it's not that one is 'right' and the rest are wrong, it's simply an illustration of how our personal experience shapes our response to and understanding of each situation.

For example, it's completely possible that while I saw them as being scared, and I saw myself as being relaxed and comfortable with the drive – they might have perceived my lack of fear as carelessness or impatience.

Are you seeing now how we each create our own reality? Or rather, our version of reality is constructed within our own mind, based on several factors, the main ones of which are:

- Past personal experiences
- Physical state (hunger, fatigue, comfort, etc.)
- Emotional state (sad, happy, etc.)
- Learned morals, ideas and beliefs

So each and every event that happens in our life is processed through our experiences, physical and emotional state, and our morals, ideas, and beliefs learned through society, family, and education.

Same Person, Same Situation, Different Mood

To further illustrate this point (because it's super important!) I'll show you how different the perception of a situation can be just by changing *one* of the elements I listed above.

Situation 1: I wake up on a Saturday morning. I had an early Friday night and woke up feeling refreshed and ready to start the day. I put on my favorite jeans, a quick swipe of makeup, my worn-in pleather jacket, and I leave the house to grab a coffee and a bagel with a pep in my step. I arrive at the coffee place and open the door. Someone looks up at me and I smile at them. They smile back and continue eating. I get to the counter, and the shop is out of bagels. The barista apologizes. I smile, tell them it's not a problem, and choose a cookie instead. I pay and walk home, stopping to smell the roses, and revel in what a beautiful morning it has been so far. I'm enjoying my cookie and reflect on how in retrospect it actually seems perfect that they didn't have my favorite bagel because the cookie happens to add a little extra sweetness on an already sweet morning.

Situation 2: I wake up on a Saturday morning. I was out late the night before with some friends, drinking and dancing until 4 a.m. My head is pounding, and all I can think about is a coffee and a bagel to help this hangover. I see myself in the mirror. Makeup smeared, hair in disarray, wearing sweats and a t-shirt. "F*ck it. I'm going like this." I say to my 'self' and drag myself out the door. I arrive at the coffee place and open the door. Someone looks up at me and this time I scowl at them thinking 'What the F are you looking at?' They turn away and continue eating. "A**hole," I mumble as I walk to the counter. I find out the shop is out of bagels. The barista apologizes. "How can you be out of F-ing bagels? Arrrrgh", I let out a frustrated moan. "Just forget it. Just give me the coffee," I bark. I pay and walk home, stomach growling from hunger, and my mind racing with angry thoughts. "What a crappy way to start the day," I think, as I drag myself home, still hungry, and now mad at the world.

When you compare the two situations, everything external was exactly the same. The people in the coffee shop, the fact that they were out of bagels, and the person looking at me when I entered. The only thing that changed was how I perceived it all. In the first situation I was happy, well-rested, and feeling positive about the day. In the second, I wasn't feeling quite so happy. And that was enough to completely change my perception of each event and of course, how I reacted to it.

Simply based on my energy levels and mood, I created two completely different realities out of the same chain of external events.

Facts vs. Stories

The reason that there are three sides to every story is because humans love to attach meaning to everything that happens. We do it naturally.

Someone looks at you when you feel good, and you're in your favorite outfit? You think, "Damn, I'm lookin' sexy today!"

Someone looks at you when you feel like crap, and you're in your worst and oldest clothes? You think, "What are they looking at? As if you don't go out in your sweats sometimes!"

Both of those are stories based around an external event, or what we'll call here a 'fact'.

The only fact (or true event/action) in the last example was that someone looked at you.

That's the entirety of what happened.

Anything else you feel or think about that situation is a *story* that you've created in your mind about what you think that might mean, based on … yep, you guessed it … your past personal experiences, your physical and emotional states, and/or your learned morals, ideas, and beliefs.

Now let's take it deeper.

Perhaps in this situation you're dying to know *why* this person looked at you, so you choose to ask them. Their answer is, "The color of your shirt caught my eye."

So now the fact of this matter is that the person looked at you because the color of your shirt caught their eye. Right?

Well not exactly.

That's still a story.

The *facts* are: Someone looked at you. You asked them, "Why did you just look at me?" And they said, "The color of your shirt caught my eye."

Those are the *only* facts. You have no way of knowing if their answer was the true reason they looked at you, or if that's just what they chose to say.

Make sense?

We are constantly creating stories and attaching meaning to external events all throughout our day.

Imagine your romantic partner is supposed to call at three o'clock, but it's now four o'clock and they still haven't called. What story will you choose to create? Is it that they don't respect you? They're cheating on you? Something bad happened to them? They're running late? They forgot? They got caught up at work? They're going to break up with you?

If you're insecure in the relationship for whatever reason, you might jump to something like 'They're cheating on me!' Or on the opposite end, perhaps you think 'They probably got caught up at work'. If you've ever been in this situation, what's your first thought? How often are you able to have this situation happen without attaching *any* meaning to it? Simply saying 'They didn't call at three o'clock.'?

Now I'll invite you to pause for a moment. Put the book down and think of a situation that happened today or recently. Can you decipher which parts are facts? And which parts are the story that you created around those facts?

The Importance of Separating Stories from Facts

The majority of our communication, both internal (that voice in your head) and external, is based on the stories we've created about situations that have happened. My guess would be that about 90% of what we say or think is a story. Even if the story is fleeting.

Which means for example that 90% of the time, when we tell a loved one about our day, we're telling them our perception of a chain of events (facts). We've grown up accustomed to making our stories interesting, to express our emotions and internal dialogue, and frankly, it typically feels pretty good to express to others how events made us feel throughout the day.

However, we're simply telling stories.

I've been telling you lots of stories already in this book! And it would be far less interesting if I chose instead to say, "One day I decided to travel. I saved up money. I went there. Then I wanted to stay so I got a new job. I stayed for another five years. Then I went home."

There isn't a lot of opportunity for connection in that story, which means that it's difficult for you to relate to the situation, and thus learn from what I'm trying to tell you. And that's why I add in more details about how I felt, about what I experienced, so that you, as the reader, can relate to me, understand me, and connect with me. I'm giving you *my perception of these events* because telling stories can be a valuable and powerful method of communication. But all of this *is* simply my perception and response to external events. As it is with any book you read, or when your friend tells you about their day. Which is why it's always so important to not simply take everything you hear from others at face value. Challenge it!

And because we spend most of our lives *telling ourselves these stories too* (on repeat, I might add), it's even more important that we challenge our own stories too.

Fun fact:

> *Humans think, on average, up to 60,000 thoughts per day. Which is approximately one thought per waking second. And the crazy part about that, is that for most people, 95% of those thoughts are repetitive, and 80% are negative.*

#MindBlownRight

We literally go around telling ourselves negative things on repeat all day, and then wonder why we're stressed, scared, overwhelmed, anxious, etc.

And guess what … *all of those negative thoughts are stories.*

An event in and of itself can't actually be negative or positive. The negative or positive spin comes only with the story that you're telling yourself.

For example:

One day I was driving my mom's car to college while mine was in the shop. Another student hit the side of the car while I was driving in the parking lot and damaged it beyond repair. I was freaking out. I kept thinking, "My mom's going to be so upset! I feel so stupid!" I had to go to the police station, file a report, call insurance, all that stuff – and when I finally called my mom to tell her that the car was damaged beyond repair, the first thing she asked me was if I was okay. Of course I was, and with relief in her voice, she said, "So, the car is totaled? That's great news! I hate that car!"

All I could do was laugh.

We both received the same news. I deemed it negative. My mom deemed it positive.

MY STORY: I was so stupid to get hit by another car, my mom's going to be so upset, and I'm such a failure.

MY MOM'S STORY: Woohoo! I get another car at the expense of my insurance!

FACTS: Two people were driving a car, one of them was me. The front of the other car went into the side of the car I was driving. The car I was driving is no longer drivable.

Are you pickin' up what I'm puttin' down here?

Do you see why is this such an important concept?

These thoughts, these stories that we tell ourselves are literally shaping our reality. How often have you spent hours or even days worrying about something happening, and then it never happens? You were creating a reality of fear and worry and anxiety over some thoughts of what *'might'* happen in the future.

And these thoughts are causing physiological changes within us too.

Remember that FFF response I was talking about?

The fact is that our brain can't tell the difference between what's real, and what's imagined. So when we create these stories, and say negative things to ourselves on repeat all day, our brain views that as a threat or attack. And so it sets off the FFF response, sending cortisol and adrenaline into our body, elevating our stress levels, which means we're more easily triggered, and we

Our brain can't tell the difference between what's real, and what's imagined.

enter into a vicious cycle of more and more stress (#chronicstress #anxiety #depressiontoo). When the FFF response is activated we perceive stress more often and more strongly because it's already fired up and we're 'on edge', looking for danger.

When we can learn to separate the story from the facts, life becomes a lot simpler. It becomes a lot less stressful, and a lot easier to manage.

And when we can see the facts as separate from the stories, we can choose what we make those facts mean. And if we're choosing, we're going to choose the stories that create our *best* life instead of worst life ... right?

One last example: If you go to an interview for a job you really want and you don't get the job, you could make it mean that you're a failure, that they didn't like you, that you're never going to get what you want in life, and in turn fire up that FFF response. *Or,* you could make it mean that you didn't get that job because something better is coming along, and you can feel hopeful and positive instead.

Either way, you didn't get the job. But which story will create a more helpful attitude moving forward? Which story will you tell yourself that will keep you motivated to continue on that job search? Is it better to show up to your next interview feeling like a failure? Or feeling like your perfect job is still out there waiting for you?

Key Takeaway

We create our reality each and every moment of each and every day. These stories we tell ourselves directly affect the way that we show up in the world, how people respond to us, and what unfolds for us on this life's path.

Just as we wake up each day to the choices we made before, we must wake up each moment to what we choose to be our reality moment by moment.

I'm curious … What reality are you creating for yourself? Is it working *for you*? Or *against you*?

> *We create our reality each and every moment of each and every day.*

CHAPTER 2

Stay Open – The Universe Has Your Back

I SPENT SIX WEEKS becoming familiar with the beaches in the South of Thailand. I slept in floating bungalows where monkeys swing from branch to branch in the towering trees on the sides of the surrounding white cliffs. I partied at one of the infamous Full Moon Parties on Koh Phangan, stayed up past dawn on Khao San Road, and lounged in hammocks on islands and ferry boats alike.

It was now July 2011, and I'd been travelling Thailand for over a month when I first made it to the famous northern city of Chiang Mai. Nestled at the base of beautiful rolling green mountains, and filled with more than three hundred exotic temples, this ancient city instantly stole my heart. The tour group I'd been travelling with, Free and Easy Traveler, had booked us in at Libra Guesthouse. Tucked into Soi 9 (Lane 9) off the main road surrounding the old city, Libra Guesthouse was (and is) a beautiful tropical oasis amidst the city's bustle of *tuk-tuks*, motorbikes, street vendors, and packs of boisterous tourists.

We were greeted by Dao, whom I later lovingly referred to as 'my Thai mom'. She checked our passports and gave us our room keys, all the while laughing and joking, poking sarcastic fun at the group. I adored her straight away.

I dropped my bag in my shared room on the second level, which overlooked a beautiful garden with stone tables, the tops carved into checkerboards and a bowl of bottle caps to be used as checker pieces. Amongst the tables, hammocks were tied from tree to tree, surrounded by lush tropical greens towering up toward the hot sun and providing shade for those in the garden below.

It was a beautiful oasis in the middle of the city, and it was calling to me to grab my book and settle into a hammock shaded by the towering palms.

But I had no time for that. Our tour manager had planned a group trip to Wat Phra That Doi Suthep. I'd already been to a couple of famous temples in Bangkok and wasn't super keen on seeing yet another one. However, I was told that the sunset from the lookout point would be more than worth the journey. And so I joined the group as we piled into a *songthaew*[1] for a ride up the mountain.

On our way to the temple, we laughed and joked about the motion sickness most of us were feeling combined with the fear of falling out the open back of the songthaew as the road curved and climbed up the steep mountain to where Wat Phra That is nestled into the mountainside at an elevation of 1,073 meters (3,520 feet). When

---

1 Songthaews are a form of public transportation in Thailand. They're essentially pick-up trucks where the bed has been customized to have two rows of seats, and there is a roof on top.

the truck finally stopped, we fell over each other as we hurriedly piled out the back, honestly more in excitement that the drive was over, rather than arriving at our destination.

And as luck would have it, just as we piled out of the truck, a wondrous Thai rainstorm blew in. For those of you who have not experienced a rainstorm in Thailand, it most often happens quickly, even unexpectedly, and quite vigorously too. From the moment you notice the dark clouds rolling in, you have but just a few moments to take cover before a torrential downpour begins. And so just as we arrived at the base of the breathtaking staircase (both literally and figuratively) lined with ornate serpent carvings and offering 309 steps to reach the temple at the top, the rain began to pour down upon us. And my-oh-my, was she a torrential downpour! But because we wanted to reach the top before the evening sunset (if the storm would indeed pass in time to allow us the view), we began to climb the stairs despite the rain.

And in all honesty, I was terrified. I used to have an incredible fear of stairs. And here was a set of 309 stairs, made of slippery tile that was now covered in the rain that continued to pelt us. My desire to see the temple had been lacking before we left, and now it had reached a place of near non-existence. However, the group wasn't stopping. So, I took off my flip-flops (my bare feet offered a much better grip) and went slowly up that staircase, one foot in front of the other, all 309 stairs until I reached the top. My breath was shaky both from exertion and from fear. Just one of the moments in my life that I pushed through the fear to find an incredible reward on the other side.

We paid our admission fee of fifty *baht* and walked inside the open-air temple. The torrential downpour was over as quickly as it had come; it was now a mere drizzle. It had lasted long enough, however, that there was scarcely a person to be found inside the open air temple other than our group. Knowing now how busy that temple normally is I look back on that evening as an incredible gift. The temple was still and quiet, but for the light rustling of the leaves and the faint, delicate chime of the small brass bells hung near the main pagoda.

Knowing little about the temple other than it was built in 1386 and is one of the most cherished and famous temples in the north, I was surprised to find I had such an instant attraction to this place once inside. I couldn't quite place my finger on what it was, but there was something inexplicably remarkable about this place. I could feel it in my soul. I was called to explore alone, and I distanced myself from the group. My flip-flops still in hand, my bare feet connecting with the smooth red tiles slippery from the rain, I barely avoided a fall by gripping the tiny patches of rough concrete with my toes as I walked. I breathed in the fresh, cool air the rain had brought in and a smile spread across my face. I suddenly felt as though a blanket of happiness had been wrapped around my shoulders. My eyes were wide with a child-like innocence and pure joy and gratitude were beaming from every inch of my body and soul. There was an indescribable energy in the air that day, and in that moment, on the top of a mountain in the north of Thailand, I knew that I was exactly where I was supposed to be. I knew that everything that had happened in my life up to that point was exactly what was meant to happen, because it had brought me to this place at this time. I felt the purest joy within me as I wandered the temple in silence, eventually perching myself at the railing overlooking Chiang Mai below and admiring the difference between the two worlds: the bustling city below and the calmness of where I stood in that moment.

With no concept of how much time had passed, I was brought out of my joyful trance when I was tapped on the shoulder by a group member letting me know we were heading back down. I reluctantly turned my gaze from the beautiful view of the city below to join the group. And with a glance over my shoulder as we took the first of the 309 steps back down the temple stairs, I knew in my heart that I would be back. I knew in my heart that this place held something for me. I didn't then know how, but I knew that its message would reveal itself to me just as it should when the time was right.

In the following five years, I ended up living at the base of that mountain, in the city of Chiang Mai. I could see the temple from below on any clear day, and I would visit it a few times a year with friends to take in the beautiful view from that same railing I stood at that first day. During that time, I never fully knew what this place had in store for me, just that it was going to be something life changing.

The Theories Behind Chapter 2

I have a saying that I live by:

"The universe is always speaking ... and it's our job to listen."

People often miss the universe's messages because:

- They think a sign has to be some grandiose gesture like a strike of lightning or a near-death experience
- They don't believe the universe sends messages in the first place
- They do receive the message but they brush it off as a 'weird feeling', or talk themselves out of believing in it
- Their mind is too darn busy overthinking, worrying, and being scared that they don't even notice

Some people call what I'm referring to as Spirit, Source, energy or one of many gods. I'm going to call it the universe, and you can choose to call it whatever you like too. The important thing is to recognize that there is a force 'out there' that is greater than all of us. And it is gently guiding us to greatness – if we let it.

It's Not Luck ... It's Action, Patience, and Universal Guidance

People have told me many times over the years that I'm lucky: I'm lucky to have had the opportunity to travel; I'm lucky to have gotten excellent jobs despite heavy competition; I'm lucky to have the people in my life that I do. And sometimes I do feel lucky. But more than luck, I feel grateful. I feel supported by the universal energy, which has guided me along the path I've taken thus far in life.

The incredible Will Smith once said,

*"Just decide what it's gonna be, who you're gonna
be, and how you're gonna do it. And then from that
point, the universe will get out of your way."*

Because we are all intricately connected to and through the universe, *everything* and *anything* can become possible when we choose
to take full responsibility for ourselves and our lives, and simultaneously lean into and trust the universal powers that be.

Unfortunately, we often get in our own way.

As humans, we spend a lot of our time thinking about what could
or might happen instead of actually declaring what *will* happen,
and then taking action. Think about a time when you liked someone and all you could think about was kissing them, or telling them
how you felt, or asking them out on a date. How much time did
you spend actually kissing, telling, or asking them on a date vs. the
time spent thinking about doing one of those things, and then the
multitude of responses they could possibly give you?

Or perhaps you wanted to apply for a job, call a potential client
with an offer, or bargain with someone at a yard sale. So often the
thinking about the multitude of possible responses from the other
party stops us from taking action. We become paralyzed in fear of
looking stupid or like a failure in front of others.

Rabbits don't waste away the day wondering what will happen if
they go out in the forest to try to find food. No way! They just get
up and go for it!

A dog doesn't stop himself from licking your face in excitement when you walk in the door because he's scared you'll think he's gross or silly. No way! He does it because that's what he wants to do!

But humans are different.

Our ego, or egoic mind, very often stops us in our tracks.

Getting to Know Your Egoic Mind

Our egoic mind is a large part of what sets humans apart from other animals in our kingdom. And it is also responsible for a large portion of human suffering, pain, and even war and violence. The ego is the part of the mind that is responsible for personal identity and self-awareness. It's largely focused on how you perceive yourself to be in the outside world, and how the outside world perceives you.

It's your identification as a Canadian, American, or Brit. It's your identification as a Chicago Bears fan, or as a teacher or a salesperson. It's also that little voice you hear wanting to be recognized for something you've accomplished, or the voice that feels hurt when someone else says the exact same idea you were *thinking* of saying but didn't. And then everyone in the room congratulates *them* for such a grand idea. It's the voice you hear of fear and jealousy when you're with your romantic partner and someone who is incredibly gorgeous starts flirting with them in front of you. It's that little voice that tells you how awesome you are – and it's also the little voice that tells you that you're a disappointment, or that nobody likes you. It's the voice that tells you you're fat, you're gorgeous, you're stupid, you're brilliant, you're a procrastinator, or you're not good at sports. It's what makes you feel like you're not good enough when you see someone you think is prettier, smarter, bigger, smaller, whiter, blacker, hairier, less hairy, taller, shorter.

It's how you identify yourself with respect to the world around you.

And the ego is sensitive.

Everyone in this world wants to be liked, or at least to not look stupid. It's part of our human condition. If you think back to when we relied on being part of a tribe to survive, it was important that we weren't outcast from the tribe, forced to try to survive on our own. These days, you can go out and get your own job, your own place, and survive fairly easily on your own. But back in our primitive days we relied on our tribes. We needed someone to do the hunting, others to do the gathering, and others still to stay back to care for the settlement, the kids, and to prepare for the food and supplies that were to be brought back. Not to mention there's safety in numbers.

Despite our advancements in survival, we still carry this need to be liked and to fit in.

And despite our advancements in survival, we still carry this need to be liked and to fit in. And so our egoic mind is constantly comparing us to others, and judging our actions, thoughts and behaviors. Unfortunately, the ego can be a very sensitive little thing, and it often gets hurt and wounded, and holds on to grudges. It often berates you for doing things wrong, or not doing things good enough. It's almost like parents who expect you to excel in sports, math, drama club, and debate club all at once while also cooking dinner for the family at night.

And it also gets easily offended.

When we find ourselves feeling offended, attacked, challenged, or defeated, it's likely that you've identified with your ego in that moment.

Your ego wants to be liked. Or rather, your ego wants *you* to be liked.

Did you catch what I just said there between the lines?

> *Your ego wants you to be liked.*

You are not your ego. But your ego is a *part* of you.

So throughout this book (and life), I want you to get used to talking to your ego and challenging it. Those little voices in your head? Yeah, you're not crazy. It's either your thinking mind or your egoic mind having a chat with you. Telling you things. And then you have the opportunity to choose to believe them or not.

Your Thinking Mind vs. Egoic Mind

Your mind is a very valuable tool. It's what allows you to read this book, to solve problems, and remember how to cook your favorite recipes. And it's also responsible for self-doubt, judgment, worry, anxiety, fear, and so much more that *isn't* helpful.

As I said above, our ego is the part of the mind that gives us our personal identity within the world we live in. Our thinking mind (sometimes called Intellect) is what allows us to solve problems, create plans, and think things through. And then there's our reactive mind that smells something on the stove and says, "Mmmm, smells good!" Essentially, three areas of the mind that respond to life in different ways.

Your ego can help you understand the world around you and help you move through with ease. It can also create fear of judgment, increase

> *Too often we allow the mind to use us, instead of us using the mind.*

self-doubt, fear, and anxiety that keep you from doing things in life for the fear of looking stupid or failing.

Your thinking mind is a great problem solver. But sometimes it becomes overrun with overthinking, worry, stress, anxiety, fear, etc. Sometimes it simply can't let things go and continues to think about certain things on repeat despite what feels like you trying everything to make it stop.

The mind in all its pieces is a valuable tool. But too often we allow the mind to use us, instead of us using the mind. If this seems weird, confusing, or like it's making your brain hurt – please, just keep reading.

For now, we're going to focus mainly on the ego. Each of us has an ego and our ego wants us to be liked. And so in turn it's very hard on us, trying to ensure that we're liked. The problem is, it has a very narrow view of the world, because it only knows what *you've* experienced.

Perhaps when you were young, your parents – often the only adult humans you cared (or knew) about – told you that you were worthless. The ego felt hurt. And if you're not taught how to appropriately deal with this emotional distress, your ego can latch on to this situation for life.

So what does that look like?

It could look like you're constantly trying to please other people and prove your worthiness. Perhaps you constantly put others in front of yourself, and you wind up one day much older, nothing to your name because you lived your life trying to please others. Alternatively, you might be so hellbent on proving your worth that you become 'successful' on the outside with money, property, etc. – but you never truly feel satisfied because that will only come when your *parents* tell you that you've succeeded. Which they may never do.

You could also go another way where you choose not to prove anything at all because instead you just adopt the idea that you truly *are* worthless and accept it as a fact. You therefore never try to do anything of importance or please others because what's the point? You already have deemed yourself worthless. Perhaps you sell yourself when you don't want to or take jobs or find yourself in situations you find degrading, or perhaps you enter abusive relationships or allow people to treat you like crap because that's all you've come to believe you're worth.

And the wild paradox is that the more you adopt this belief that you're worthless, the more you start to see evidence of that, and the more you relate to it and accept it as who you are. Your ego hears 'you're worthless' and continues to find evidence in your life that supports that. It shows up in your mind over and over again: "You're worthless." "You're not good enough." "You'll never be enough."

And only when you can see those sentences for what they truly are – random thoughts that you've attached to – you can finally let them go.

Our Ego Builds Its Defense System as We Grow Older

As we grow up, we are taught different things about our identity. We are taught ideas and beliefs from our parents about the world, about who they are, and about ourselves. We're taught ideas and beliefs from social media, movies, TV, fashion magazines, and advertisements. As we grow up, we gain this perception of our own identity and where we fit inside this world, or external reality.

For example, we are surrounded by media outlets. If everyone depicted in movies, TV, and other forms of media and advertisements are all young, white, fit, and have lots of hair – and we aren't young, white, fit, with lots of hair – our ego will most definitely notice that. It will notice that one of these things is not like the other. And if that external reality doesn't match how you see yourself, you'll start to feel badly about yourself, feel the need to conform, think you're not good enough and so on. The ego will have you start to believe that you don't fit into the tribe, that you're not good enough, white enough, fit enough, full head of hair enough, and it will continue to tell you these things if you let it.

But, you have the power to rise above the ego's perceptions of your world. It isn't always easy, especially at first. But it can absolutely be done.

And the first step is to understand that your ego is its own entity.

From the moment you're born to the moment you die your ego is collecting information about the world around you. And it will try to get you to conform to the status quo. It's not just looking at the physical aspects of the world, it picks up on culture, beliefs of your parents, church group, or the media and social media. It listens to the conversations of the people at the grocery store while you're shopping, and it gains information from books, studies, or whatever you immerse yourself in. It paints a giant picture of the world for you, and how you relate to it, and who you are in it.

And while it has its positive qualities to help you understand the world as you move through it, there are times where it does you *no favors*.

In fact, in some cases it can be quite detrimental to your joy, happiness, and success in life.

Which is why it's so important to be the watcher of the egoic mind, be the watcher of the thinking mind, so that you detach yourself from the ego's thoughts and beliefs when it benefits you to do so. Just because the mind thinks it, doesn't mean you have to believe it or adopt it as your truth.

There is immense power in separating yourself from the ego, because when you do that you can become whoever you want to be. You can be confident, happy, joyful, successful, worthy, and so much more.

Notice as Your Ego Gets Offended and Choose to Stay Open

Your ego has developed a sense of identity for you. It has provided you with certain beliefs, which you've adopted as your own, and you live out life from those beliefs.

One example is a parent leaving a child at a young age. The child creates a story in their mind that their parent left because they're unlovable. And as they grow older, they start to see more and more evidence of this. Perhaps they don't get chosen as someone's partner for a project in school – and the ego says, 'See? You're unlovable.' And then they get older, and they start dating, and their partner says they can't hang out that night because they're going out with friends. And the ego says, 'See? You're unlovable.' And so it goes.

Now, one might challenge that ego's conclusion and say that the fact they *have* a partner lends itself to the fact that they *are* lovable at least to some degree, but that's not how the ego works when left to its own devices. It will lock into the belief it created when you were a child and find evidence throughout life to support that.

And so as this person in the example gets older, they will continue to see evidence of being unlovable until one day they wake up and decide to challenge the ego. And boy oh boy, the ego will fight back.

And that's what might happen to you as you continue to read this book.

Your beliefs and ideas about life might be challenged. When you realize that the decades you spent living in a state of fear, anxiety, sadness, or pain can be 'fixed' on your own simply by challenging your ego and your thinking mind – it's a new reality that might feel difficult to accept.

As you start to understand that it has been *you* creating a self-made prison all along – that someone may have done something to you when you were five, or 15, or 25 – but now it's

> *The solution to your sadness, anxiety, worry, shame, or self-doubt is and always has been within you.*

simply living in your head as a memory and a belief that you created around that situation. It's *you*, not that person that allows it to continue to affect your life. And your ego isn't going to accept that easily.

Your ego isn't going to want to hear that the solution to your sadness, anxiety, worry, shame, or self-doubt is and always has been within you. Your ego isn't going to want to hear that the only person who has been keeping you from living your dream life is you. And so your ego may want to fight the words and ideas on these pages.

And that, my friends, is progress.

I invite you to be open to challenging your ego and its beliefs as you continue to read this book. Notice what is triggering for you, and notice what makes you say, 'That's bull crap', and what makes you angry, and what makes you feel happy.

Notice what thoughts are coming up and do your best to simply watch them instead of attaching to them or even believing them.

If you think, 'This is annoying', try saying it in a way that acknowledges yourself as separate from the thinker. For example, 'This sentence has triggered thoughts and feelings of annoyance,' or simply, 'That thought told me that I am annoyed.'

It might seem strange to you now if you're not used to the process, but I'm going to ask you to try to adopt it at least while you're reading this book.

And adopt it out there in the world while you're reading this book too! Perhaps you're the type of person who thinks, 'Bad things always happen to me.' Instead, wake up in the morning and say what Dr. Shauna Shapiro always says, 'I wonder what wonderful things will happen to me today?' And just notice how you might see your external world change.

Because as we learn to separate ourselves from the thoughts in the mind – and instead to notice the thoughts as they arise without attachment – we can begin to change these thoughts. We can begin to change them to something more positive and create more space within the mind to create a more positive life.

For now, let your ego fight with you. Notice what it tries to tell you and ask yourself if what it says is helpful for you or not. Because that's when we can take back the control over our life. We get to choose how we respond to situations, people, and our thoughts.

And this allows us to open ourselves up to new ideas, new practices, new ways of life, and new ways of *being*, which of course in turn opens us up to new possibilities to create our best life.

And as we continue to separate ourselves from the thinker, we open ourselves up to the guidance of the universe. When I was up there on the mountain that first visit, I had such a deep knowing that it held something truly spectacular for me. And I had no idea what that was, and I had no idea when it would take place. But I didn't attach myself to these thoughts, I didn't obsess over them, I didn't try to figure out what, when, or why. I was able to simply let the knowing be.

We tend to spend too much time in our thoughts, overrun by the ego.

It's so important to challenge the ego, quiet the ego, and incorporate an embodied experience of life through the guidance of the universe. Because this is the difference between people who have what they truly want in this world, and the people who don't. It's the difference between the people who seem 'lucky' and the people who don't.

My life hasn't always been *easy*, but I have been able to quiet the egoic mind, detach from the meanings that my mind tries to give 'negative' situations and follow the guidance of the universe instead.

Quieting the Ego to Turn Up the Volume of the Universe

Have you ever felt an urge to do something and then talked yourself out of it?

I'm going to encourage you to talk yourself *into it* a little more often.

For example, let's look again at when I was twenty-three years old, working a full-time job, partying every weekend, and going to school for Image Consulting in the evenings. My teacher, Karen Brunger, recommended that we read the book *The Power of Now* by Eckhart Tolle. There I was, all coked up sitting in a class to learn about fashion, living a highly superficial lifestyle, feeling a wee bit baffled when Karen started teaching us about human beings as energy. I was there to learn about fashion and image – not energy, right?! It was the first time I'd heard anything about us being bundles of energy that respond and react to each other, not to mention that our mind can control much of this energy.

It was truly a foreign concept to this party gal.

And as I sat there in that class, there was a part of me that questioned everything she said, thinking that it couldn't possibly be real (oh hello, ego!). And another part of me that felt really intrigued to learn more about what she was talking about. The latter was a more embodied, gut feeling that I needed to learn about what she was saying. Despite what my ego was telling me *ahem* this is bullshit *ahem* I decided to follow my gut and I purchased and read the book later that week.

And holy shit! It changed my life.

Despite the fact that it was a very overwhelming and at times intimidating book, I read the entire thing, taking from it whatever I could.

Had I listened to my ego telling me the teacher was a bit cray cray, instead of listening to my gut, I don't even want to imagine how different my life would be today.

And this is a perfect example of a small nudge I received from the universe. Pay attention to what your ego is fighting you on, because there's a good chance whatever it's fighting is exactly what you need to make a change in your life.

Key Takeaway

Please, stay present with me. Allow your ego to fight back. Don't get caught up in your mind if some things I say don't make sense to you. And just enjoy the ride, knowing that each time your ego gets angry, defensive, or aggravated – it simply means you're opening yourself up to a new way of thinking, a new way of being, and of course new possibilities in your life.

> *Stay present with me. Allow your ego to fight back.*

CHAPTER 3

Letting Go of Resistance

"I DON'T WANT TO leave. I don't want to leave. I don't want to leave."

The thought repeated itself in my mind over and over as I sat in the lobby of the Wild Orchid Guesthouse in late August of 2011. My backpack sat filled to the brim beside me, as I waited for the van to arrive that would take me to the airport for my flight out of Thailand.

It had been just two months since I'd first stepped out of that cab in front of the Wild Orchid – my very first experience of Thailand – but it felt like a lifetime ago. I had grown more in those two months than I felt I'd grown in the entire decade before. The people, the places, the cultures I'd seen – I would never be the same person again. And I had no desire to be.

A journal entry from August 8th, 2011 – written the day I visited a landmine and war museum in Cambodia – shows just one example of how my experiences were shaping me each and every day:

> Our guide at the war museum told us how he lost his arm by a land mine … He also lost his mother and father to a landmine when he was 14, and his brother and sister a few years later. By comparison, 'only' losing his one arm made him the lucky one in his family … Now that he is an amputee, he is a second tier citizen and finds it very difficult to find a job … Leaving this man I just met today filled me with such emotion and I realized just how lucky I really am. At that moment, I wanted that feeling to stay with me always. To always remember how little I need to survive, and how lucky I am to have what I do. I wish everyone back home could see and experience what I experienced today. It would truly make it such a better place. It is going to be so hard to go back home and watch all the waste, the materialism, etc.

I wasn't the same person who'd arrived in 'The Land of Smiles' earlier that year, and the thought of leaving this country, this area of the world, that I'd come to fall in love with felt heavy. And I also knew that my next adventure was awaiting me.

I was leaving Thailand yes, but not for home. I was headed to Australia. A place I'd been dying to go, and a place for which I'd acquired a one-year working holiday visa. For my next adventure, I planned on spending a year working and living Down Under. It was something I'd wanted to do for so long, and yet there was this nagging feeling in the pit of my stomach that was telling me I wasn't done in Thailand. And I also knew that if I didn't see Australia when I had the chance (not to mention my friend waiting to pick me up from the airport on the other side) that I'd regret it later on.

So with a heavy heart for a country I knew I'd miss dearly, and a trust in the universe that my path would undoubtedly unfold before me just as it should, I boarded the plane and away I went.

Exploring Down Under

Turns out, a week in Perth with a dear friend, Brad, whom I'd met in Los Angeles a few years before was exactly what I'd needed to bring the joy back into my adventure. The two of us ate amazingly delicious Western-style food that I hadn't realized how much I'd missed while in Asia. We fed kangaroos in a petting zoo and watched wild ones hopping home in massive herds across the fields as the sun set behind them. We walked in parks full of giant trees, we talked and laughed until we cried, and I was honored by an invitation to his childhood home for a home-cooked meal with his parents and boyfriend. After months of backpacking, it felt good to be home, even if it wasn't my own.

And after a week of good times, I found myself back on a plane, this time to Melbourne.

Ah, Melbourne. What a beautiful, hip, fun city.

And after spending so much time in Southeast Asia … it sure felt EXPENSIVE too!

The cheapest hostel I'd found was Nations Hostel by Flinders Street Station priced at AUD$36 per night for a 12-bed dorm. As I handed my credit card over to the receptionist in the front lobby of the old Victorian home turned hostel, all I could think about were the 5-star accommodations a price like that could get me back in Thailand.

It was a cute hostel, with a huge kitchen table where all of us wild nomads met each day for dinner and/or a game of cards or dice as we shared among us the cheapest *bags* of wine and the free pasta supplied by the hostel.

If you've ever spent a prolonged period of time in a hostel, you'll know how interesting these places can be. And what an amazing group of characters you'll meet from all walks of life. I laugh at my journal entry from August 30th, 2011:

> I have met a few funny characters in the hostel, such as ass-hole Joe, drunken John, Paul who cooks for everyone, Derek the Scottish guy who works in the kitchen, the "American" who insisted me and the other Joe should be hooking up, the family that seemed a little TOO close, and the Asian family who wouldn't stop crinkling the bags at 3 a.m.

As I read that aloud I can picture each one of them gathered around the table. And while I was having a good time at that hostel, I also wasn't able to shake the feeling that it wasn't where I was meant to be. Aside from the incredible accent, Melbourne felt so similar to Toronto but without any of the home comforts of friends and family. I began to feel that if I was going to spend a year abroad, I wanted to spend it somewhere unique. I wanted to experience something I'd never experienced before: new cultures, new languages, exotic food, and whatever else you could throw my way.

My body was in Melbourne, but my heart was in Chiang Mai. As I entertained the idea of going back to Chiang Mai instead of getting a job and staying in Melbourne, I was met with a flood of combative thoughts.

"What about my working holiday visa? I paid for it already, and soon I'll be too old to get a new one."

"And this was my plan! I can't go back on my plan, can I?"

"What would people think?"

"How would I even support myself in Chiang Mai without a work visa like I had in Australia?"

But after a few days, my internal compass won the battle.

I followed my gut and booked a flight back to Chiang Mai through Bangkok.

Three weeks after landing in Melbourne, I was on my way back to the Land of Smiles. As I sat on the airplane, I wrote in my journal:

> I'm on my way back to Bangkok and I can't describe how I feel. I saw the most beautiful sunset out the plane window tonight that brought tears to my eyes. I am so happy to be going back to Asia.
>
> Life awaits.

The Theories Behind Chapter 3

It's been cited time and time again that resiliency and adaptability are two traits that all wildly successful people possess. And the great thing about that is that both of these traits can be learned.

And guess what?

This comes down once again to quieting the mind and detaching from our thoughts.

Not All Thoughts Are Your Ego

In the last chapter we talked about our egoic mind – or our identity. When beliefs are presented to us that challenge the identity that our ego has created for us, it can sometimes feel uncomfortable. But not all thoughts in our mind are considered ego.

Our ego is the identification with a thought that arises in the mind, such as 'I'm fat.' or 'I'm too stupid to get that job', or 'I'm a proud Canadian'. These are thoughts that are directly related to our identity as we perceive ourselves in this world. But let's say you experience a thought such as 'That's a loud noise!' or 'What's on the stove? It smells delicious!' or 'I should bake a cake tonight'. These are not linked with your personal identity. I refer to this simply as the 'thinking mind' and the thinking mind loves coming up with observations and ideas.

Now just like the egoic mind, the thinking mind is no angel either. Besides things like 'I'm hungry right now', it also loves to create wild stories such as those we discussed in Chapter 1. This part of your mind comes up with things like, 'Maybe Bob didn't call because he got in a car accident.' or 'What if I lose my job and suddenly I can't pay my bills?'. Anything that's not directly related to your personal identity is considered the thinking mind.

The thinking mind is responsible for creating those stories based on the facts of what happens each day.

And when we're faced with a situation that might be deemed negative, the thinking mind can go wild with stories like the ones I started creating when I thought about possibly leaving Australia and going back to Thailand instead.

Reminder:

"What about my working holiday visa? I paid for it already, and soon I'll be too old to get a new one."

And this was my plan! I can't go back on my plan, can I?"

"What would people think?"

"How would I even support myself in Chiang Mai without a work visa like I had in Australia?"

Had I allowed myself to get taken away by those thoughts of what seemed like the 'right' thing to do, versus following my gut, I might never have left. And it's a common thing in this life – people staying somewhere or staying with someone not because they want to but because they get stuck in a never ending loop of thoughts and 'reasons' why they can't make that change.

Which is why being able to adapt to new situations – and bounce back from crappy ones quickly – are important skills when it comes to achieving what you want in life.

Resistance vs. Adaptability and Resilience

Something I read in *The Power of Now* by Eckhart Tolle many years ago stuck with me from that moment forward. I don't remember the exact quote, and I'm sure I've altered it slightly over the years, but the idea is still there, and the idea is this:

If you have a situation in your life that is causing you pain or suffering, you have three options:

- Do nothing and continue to suffer.
- If you *can* change the situation … change it!
- If you *can't* change the situation … accept the situation as if you'd chosen it.

And now I'll invite you to read that again, because it's one of the most powerful lessons I've ever learned.

And to put some icing on that cake of powerful wisdom, Buddhism reminds us that pain is part of human life. We're treated poorly or unfairly by others, we lose those we love, we get fired from jobs we wanted to keep, we don't get accepted to the program we wanted, we stub our toe on the way to the bathroom in the middle of the night.

Pain in this human existence is inevitable.

Suffering is optional.

Suffering is caused by being in resistance to what is. It is caused by resisting, pushing away from, or not accepting your external reality. Or in other words:

Suffering = Pain x Resistance

I'll give you a (very basic) example. Let's say you bought a chocolate bar and put it in the fridge to eat after dinner, and then went about your day. After dinner you go to retrieve your treat, and it's gone! Your housemate (partner, kid, roommate, whatever) must have eaten it, and now they've gone out for the night. You suddenly get furious. 'I wanted that chocolate bar!' you start to scream in your head. 'How could they take something that's mine?! Now I have nothing left! I'm so mad!' You can feel your body physiology change, the stress hormone has been released. Perhaps you're clenching your fists, or you feel a sudden heaviness or heat in your body. You feel the anger rising within you.

And now this is where the three options come in:

Option 1: You sit down on the couch, arms crossed tightly in front of you, thinking about how that was so disrespectful of them and how angry you are. It ruined your night. Perhaps you're thinking about all the other times they've done something similar in the past, and how it made you angry then too. You start thinking about all the things you're going to say to that person when you see them next. This wonderful night you had planned – eating this delicious chocolate bar in front of your favorite TV show – has been ruined! And it's all their fault! You spend the rest of the night in a grumpy mood ruminating on all the times this person has wronged you in the past, and you have a real crappy night overall.

Option 2: You roll your eyes as the anger dissipates, and you choose to find something else in the house that you can eat for a treat. If you don't have anything else in the house, perhaps you choose to go out to the store and buy another one, or call Uber Eats to bring you something delicious. Sure, it's not what you had planned, but it's better than crying over spilled milk, right? Or in this case, crying over missing chocolate bars. You eat your substitute treat while you watch your show and go to bed content.

Option 3: You're unable (or unwilling) to do any of the things in Option 2 (maybe you don't have a car, or enough money, or it's simply too late at night) and so you say to yourself, 'It clearly wasn't meant to be tonight. I'll enjoy the chocolate bar even more tomorrow when they bring me a new one, and I've had to wait for it even longer.' And then you carry on with watching your favorite show and make the most of things as they are. The anger has dissipated, and as you head to bed you're happy with how your night went overall.

Do you see where I'm going here?

The example above is just a simple missing chocolate bar. But the overarching theme plays out in many other situations in life.

Option 1 = Resistance
Option 2 = Adaptability
Option 3 = Resilience

Often our modern human nature is to sit and ruminate on the things that hurt us, or make us worried, anxious or upset. We wallow in self-doubt, indecision, and guilt – all of which can be considered resistance to what is.

And what I hope you'll notice in this example too, is that all of the suffering you would have endured choosing Option 1 was created in your mind. It was a choice to sit and think about all the ways this person has wronged you in the past. And those thoughts created more and more anger in that moment and through the whole night.

Now some people will argue and say that those thoughts were created because that person did you wrong. That person took your chocolate bar.

And to that I say, NOT TRUE. The initial anger perhaps, yes. But after the first few thoughts, it was a choice of your own to continue to be angry.

Your response is always your choice.

What We Resist Persists

By choosing to sit and think about past things that have been done, or simply to focus on the fact that you don't currently have a chocolate bar that you really wanted – this is resisting what is. The fact of the matter is, there is no more chocolate bar. End of story. It's gone.

So will you choose to sit there and think about the fact that there's no chocolate bar? Or will you choose to accept the fact that there's no chocolate bar, and move on?

When you choose to accept that there is no chocolate bar and carry on with your night, the perceived problem quickly dissipates.

But when you instead choose to keep thinking about the chocolate bar all night, the problem continues to be part of your present moment – for as long as you continue to think about it. The more you resist accepting the fact that there's no chocolate bar, the longer the problem persists.

What we resist ... persists.

This might seem ridiculous when we're talking about a chocolate bar. Is someone over the age of five really going to stew all night about the fact that someone ate their chocolate bar? I hope not. Although with the right trifecta of stressors leading up to the event, you just never know!

However, this exact same principle applies to everything from the missing chocolate bar, to being stuck in traffic, getting fired from your job, being cheated on by your spouse, or even the loss of a loved one.

If you are unable to do anything to change the perceived problem, you have three options – resist it, adapt to it, or accept it. And very often, accepting and adapting go hand in hand. First accept, then adapt. Or sometimes it's just a matter or accepting it and moving on.

Of course - if you can *change* the situation at hand to eliminate the problem – do it!

Otherwise, you can choose to suffer from the situation *or* choose to accept it and move on, ending your suffering.

Yes, this even works when it comes to major 'problems'

You might be thinking, 'Sure, this works when you're talking about a chocolate bar, but surely you can't mean that if my dog dies I just need to accept it and move on, just like that?'

And actually, I do mean just that!

Now before you get in a tizzy, I do have a heart, and the loss of a loved one – animal or human – can be absolutely heartbreaking. And I encourage you to grieve. I actually have a Spotify playlist specifically for times when I have experienced great loss or disappointment and feel the need to grieve. I've grieved over broken relationships, the loss of loved ones, and I've even grieved the loss of my job and the life that was intertwined with it.

But I also put a structure and a timeline on it.

I do the exact opposite of resisting what is, and I just lean into the grief. I allow myself to think all the thoughts, and feel the pain, the hurt, the 'what if's and the 'should have's'. And then I move on.

I actually call this process a constructive breakdown.

For smaller grievances, I'll shut myself up in my bedroom for a few hours, my super sad playlist blasting, and curl up on the floor bawling. Sometimes I'll watch myself cry hysterically in the mirror.[2]

Instead of resisting the sadness, I lean into it as much as possible. I give myself dedicated time and space to do nothing but feel my emotions and release them. All emotions are valid. I'll usually add in some time spent journaling, and within an hour or two, I'll be feeling far more positive and energized.

Then there was the time my fiancé and I broke up, and I gave myself a full three weeks to mourn. I called my two best friends and asked them to be there for me. During that time, I was allowed to cry and complain and talk about the breakup as much as I wanted. And then I had to move on at the end. As it turned out, I didn't even take the whole three weeks before I stopped talking about it all the time and felt infinitely better.

Not to say that fleeting moments of sadness didn't occur after that, but it wasn't the crushing pain that I experienced in the beginning. And this is exactly the power of not resisting what is.

By allowing ourselves to fully feel our emotions instead of resisting them and pretending we're fine, we give them space to exit our body. Emotions are simply a build-up of energy inside of us and if we pretend they're not there, they'll persist!

Emotions are natural. Emotions are what make this human life so exhilarating! But the key to a joyful and successful existence is to not allow these emotions to take control of us for long periods of time.

Really, I'm not a heartless robot

---

2   Anyone else find that oddly satisfying? Tag me on Instagram or Facebook and let me know if you do the same! @KandisJames.KJ

I've had people make comments to me that it's not natural to just shut off my emotions. Or it's natural to feel this pain and sorrow. I've had people ask me if these practices are meant to dim our emotions or get rid of those strong feelings.

Heck no. Heck no. *Heck no!*

I feel emotions very deeply. I've just done enough training of the mind that I can release them before I get crushed under the weight of them.

Let's say for example that a loved one passes away. Of course, you're going to be sad. You're going to miss them! And it's important to take the time to grieve and get an understanding of what life is going to be like now that they're gone. (#accept #adapt) But spending months thinking of nothing but how you're going to miss them, that life isn't fair, that you weren't ready, that you can't believe it – that's not going to help anything, is it?

I'm not saying don't feel things. I'm just saying don't let yourself get caught up in a whirlwind of thoughts that keep you in a low place for extended periods of time. There's a *HUGE* difference.

Training Your Brain for Adaptability and Resilience

Whether we're talking about finding yourself in a hostel in Australia when you'd rather be in Thailand, or we're talking about getting fired from your job, or losing a loved one … your ability to adapt and be resilient comes down to your ability to recognize your thoughts as thoughts – without getting attached to them – and then tapping into your body and the universal guidance to understand your next steps forward.

It's also important to remember that emotions are simply physiological responses to your perception (also known as thoughts) of what's happening to you or around you. And as we're going to continue to see throughout this book, when something comes from a thought, we have the power to *change* the thought, because it's our own mind that created that thought in the first place!

And so once again we're back to noticing our thoughts as just that – thoughts.

We are not our thoughts.

But … our thoughts can become us. Which is why this is so important.

Our brain can't tell the difference between what we imagine in our mind, and what is happening in real life. To the brain, they're the same thing. Whether you think it or experience it, your body triggers the stress response as if it's really happening. And when we continue to get caught in this spiral of negative thoughts, the body becomes more and more stressed, which in turn creates more and more of these thought spirals, and in turn that creates a vicious cycle that can lead to depression, chronic stress, anxiety, or other mental health conditions.

Which is why it's so important to see our thoughts as thoughts – not facts.

Meditation: Watching Your Thoughts

This meditation is a shortened version of Dekyi-Lee Older-shaw's 'Clarity of Mind'.*

Bring your awareness to your breathing.

Notice the in-breath and the out-breath.

There is no need to change your breathing, simply notice it.

Now let your attention ride or float on the breath similar to the way you would float on the surface of the ocean where there are gentle waves coming and going. Now move your attention away from the breathing to the mind itself, that which is aware of breathing.

In other words, instead of being aware of the breath, which is the object of your awareness, become aware of the mind itself, the part of you that is observing the breath, experiencing the breath.

The mind is like space or like sky, completely clear, not solid, and it is vast, spacious, and unlimited.

Try to get a sense of how your mind is like this clear, vast, spacious sky.

You are this clear, vast spaciousness.

The things that you are aware of, the thoughts, images, memories and so on, are similar to the clouds that pass through the sky. They're not always there, and they are not really you but they appear or arise and after a while they disappear.

Let them come and let them go, realize that they are only momentary and not solid, they just come and go.

You might label them "thought", "sensation", "sound", or "image" when you notice them.

Then notice them going and return your awareness to the mind itself, your real nature, which is like the clear spacious sky – who you really are.

Clear, untainted, spacious.

"I am not these temporary clouds of thoughts and emotions. These are mental events, things that come and go in my mind. They are not me and not who I really am."

Rest in this and focus there for a few minutes.

For a recording of this guided meditation, go to:
kandisjames.com/watchingyourthoughts

How did that feel?

What thoughts arose for you while you read or listened to that guided meditation?

What do you now know that you didn't know before? And how will that affect the way you move forward?

Key Takeaway

When we can see our thoughts as separate from ourselves – when we can watch the thinker instead of *being one with the thinker* – so many positive changes become possible in our lives. Simply from removing our attachment to our thoughts.

Remember … we are not our thoughts.

If you have a situation in your life that is causing you pain or suffering, you have three options:

- Do nothing and continue to suffer.

- If you *can* change the situation ... change it!

- If you *can't* change the situation ... accept the situation as if you'd chosen it.

> ### *If you have a situation in your life that is causing you pain or suffering, you have three options:*

CHAPTER 4

Fear is a Creation of Your Mind

I LAID OUT MY tiger balm, notebook, playing cards, and books on the bedside table and folded my clothes up and placed them neatly beneath the shelf. Who knew that unpacking a backpack could feel so exciting?

I flopped down on my bed with a sigh of relief. I had just paid two full months of rent for this room at Libra Guesthouse, and it felt so good to have a place to call my own. It was on the main floor at the back of the guesthouse complex, and my front door opened directly into the hammock-filled garden I'd noticed on my first day in Chiang Mai a few months before. The room was fairly small, consisting of a king size bed, one bedside table, and a bathroom with a cold-water-only shower. But it only cost me about $200/month, and it was a place I could finally call my own after so many months of shared accommodation. I could spread out my stuff, read until the wee hours of the morning without disturbing anyone, and walk around naked! Heck yes!

It felt like heaven.

My Room at Libra that felt like a castle.

With a smile on my face, I peeled myself back off the bed and walked down the busy street to AUA Language School in the middle of the old city. If I was going to stay for any length of time, I wanted to be able to communicate in the local language, and it just so happened the next Thai language beginner's classes were starting in just a few days. I paid my deposit and squealed with excitement. To me, learning the language meant being able to immerse myself more fully in the culture by speaking with locals and being able to venture outside of the main cities where English is widely spoken.

In an effort to familiarize myself with my new home – even if it was temporary – I strolled down Ratvithi Road, passing by small shops, guesthouses, and food stalls that lined the street. Motorbikes seemed to be parked everywhere with no rhyme or reason to their placement, and I was so content just soaking everything in – the sights, the sounds, and the smells.

Everything was so different than it was back home. I continued to walk along until I found myself peering into a little shop called 'On the Road Books'. The front of the shop was open to the street showcasing rows and rows of used books. An older Englishman was sitting at a small table in the back, his nose buried in a book, and a small cash box sitting beside him. He noticed me walk in and asked me if I'd been in before. Of course I told him I hadn't, and he let me know that all the books were used, mainly dropped off by travelers as they passed through the city, and if I stayed long enough to finish a book he would buy it back from me for 50% of what I paid. I'd never seen anything like it, and as an avid reader on a tight budget I was in love with the concept. Each book cost between $2.00–$10.00 and I found myself visiting this man every few days to restock.

For a while, that was my life.

I lived in a small room in a guesthouse and I'd walk to language school five days a week for four hours each day. I spent a large portion of the rest of my time reading books in the hammocks outside my room, studying with the help of Dao at the guesthouse restaurant, or testing out local bars and restaurants in an attempt to meet people and make friends.

Despite my learning Thai, I was unable to read most menus on the local street food carts, and I fumbled my way through buying clothing, food, or drinks at the local markets.

Despite not being wildly busy each day, every day felt like an adventure. There was the language barrier of course, which made certain things challenging. But then there was also the food, the tastes, the smells, the culture – the way people behaved and what they did. Everything was so different. Even the way the buildings looked, what the furniture was made out of, and the flooded streets during the rainy season that were often covered in 20–30 cm (4–8 inches) of rainwater, which didn't faze anyone nearly as much I thought it should..

I would walk into a shop, and nobody would greet me. I'd order food with a friend, and both of our dishes would come out at completely different times, and sometimes they got our order right, but often they got it wrong. Nobody said anything though, we just went with it – because that's how it is over there.

Surrounded by Difference

Everything around me was different than what I'd known my whole life.

One day, I had just come home from class and I decided to sit at *Thai 1 On Bar*, which was steps away from my guesthouse at the end of the laneway. It was run by an American man who'd been there many, many years, and it was one of the first places I'd found that served decent wine.

I sat down at the table that faced out into the charming laneway full of trees, motorbikes, stray cats and dogs, and shop owners sitting on stools outside their shops watching the people pass by in the heat of the day.

The view of Soi 9 MoonMuang from Thai 1 On Bar

So there I was, sipping a glass of wine at the table that was open to and overlooking the lane, and I was reflecting on my solo travels up to that point.

Traveling solo gives a person quite a lot of time for self-reflection (and I do mean a lot of time). And as I sat there that hot Thai afternoon, I wrote and wrote and wrote in my journal. And part of what I wrote was this:

> From the day you are born, your ego begins to associate with its surroundings and experiences, aiding you in developing your sense of self.

One day, you remove yourself from everything that is familiar to you, and your ego takes a blow. It can no longer familiarize or often comprehend the people you see, the things around you, and the new experiences that are taking place. Conventional habits are not conventional in your new place, and your layers of protection that you've built over the years are slowly stripped away.

You are uncertain, you are awed, you are sometimes scared. Scared of your surroundings, scared of being so far away, and scared of being alone. So, you begin to push your limits. You start to talk to people you might not have talked to. You do things you might not have done. You eat things you might never have eaten.

And the more you push your boundaries, the faster the layers of 'normalcy' are stripped away, and you are forced to take a look at your deepest, darkest layers that hold the secrets to who you really are.

How do you act? To people? To situations? To cultures? To 'problems'? And then you look further – Why do you act that way? Is it okay?

And when these layers are stripped away to reveal your most intimate characteristics, you have to ask yourself – 'Do you like what you see? Are you who you thought you were?'

In that moment, I felt like I was finally understanding myself to a point where I could change the things I didn't like, and relish in the ones that I did. Through my travels I was seeing, getting in touch with, and learning about myself and the world in profoundly new ways.

When I tell people I travelled for so long, and lived in Thailand for so long, most people think of it as living a life on vacation. And while there was definitely time for parties, for reading and relaxing, and exploring new places, it was even more so a journey within myself. It was a journey that pushed me to face my fears and step far, far, far outside my comfort zone. It very often made me wildly uncomfortable. It very often made me wonder, 'What the heck am I doing out here?' but deep down I knew exactly why I was pushing myself. I knew that deep down I was capable of and destined for so much more than the life I'd been leading back home. I was made for more than going to the office each day, dissolving arguments between family members, and biding my time until the weekend rolled around again, just to party the weekends away and go straight back to feeling resentful on Monday morning. I needed to get away from it all and to be alone. Alone in a new country with a new language in a culture I was doing my best to understand more and more each day. I needed to meet new people with different outlooks on life and expand my understanding of how the world is.

And that's what I was doing.

I was pushing myself far beyond my comfort zone and it was scary at times, but also exhilarating.

> *When we start pushing past our comfort zone ... that is when life truly begins.*

When we start pushing past our comfort zone (that place where we live out each day doing what we always do because even if it's not exactly what we want to do, at least it's not awful) and we take chances, try new things, and put ourselves out there – that is when life truly begins.

But the reason most of us stay IN our comfort zone is because getting out of it is scary and hella uncomfortable! Hence the term 'comfort' zone. Fear of what we *might* experience keeps us in our zone. We know that it *might* turn out better than what we've got at the moment, buuuuut … it also might turn out worse. And that's *exactly* what stops most people from moving forward.

But to get where we truly want to be (and are destined to be) in this life, we've got to face those fears. We must get in touch with what we're truly scared of, and then go out there and face it. Because the only way to truly get past it is to go through it – to look our fears in the eye. And the more we do that, the more we see that we're capable of beating those fears. And with that, we learn to believe in ourselves and our ability to do bigger and scarier things.

The degree to which a fear holds you back is directly correlated with the attention you give it

Each of us have big fears and smaller fears.

We also have what could be considered internal and external fears.

We all have them. For some of us they simply show up in different ways. But at the root, all fear is the same. All fear is created by a thought.

For example, *my external fears* were:

Heights

I was insanely afraid of heights. To the point that one day I was in the mall in my early twenties, and I had looked over the railing from the third floor down to the first, and I was petrified. I literally had to get down on my hands and knees and crawl away from the railing because I felt if I had taken a regular step, the floor would have given way beneath me. (Apparently crawling is safer …

who knew?) Also, I went skydiving. Willingly and enthusiastically at that. Apparently, that doesn't count in my mind as a height – go figure.

Getting Killed

When I was in high school, I was so afraid that someone would be hiding in my closet when I got home, that I would put a VHS tape in front of the door so I'd know if someone had gone inside. I literally went inside the closet and tried for at least thirty minutes to see if I could close the door *and* somehow put the tape back where it was. And nope. It was impossible. So, every day before leaving the house I'd put the tape there and check it when I got back to my room to make sure it hadn't been moved to confirm nobody was hiding in my closet to kill me.

Public Bathrooms

I hated public bathrooms, and often feared them, for a reason I've never quite understood. And I didn't take a poop in one until I was twenty-seven years old. Seriously! In high school I'd hold it, or I'd walk home on lunch or skip class if I really had to go. The day I finally did the deed was about a month or two before I left for Thailand. I was at the Bloor Boxing Gym in Toronto at 5:30 a.m. I started my 8 km (5 miles) run on the treadmill and realized I really had to go. (Have you ever tried running while you gotta go? Not nice.) I thought about leaving the gym and going home, but I was really into my morning workouts at that time, so I didn't want to miss it. If I went home then, I wouldn't get to work out before going to the office. So, knowing I was the only female in the gym that early, I went into the locker room bathroom. And I pooped. And I was SO excited that I literally called my mom to tell her. And she was so excited too. It was a big event. Little did I know that a few months later I'd be having emergency poops in squatter toilets at roadside stops in Thailand. Talk about pushing past your comfort zone! (Good news: I now have no fear of pooping. Or talking about poop, as you can see.)

Snakes

I was hiking on the Niagara Escarpment one day with a friend in my early twenties. We sat down on the edge of the escarpment taking in the beautiful views, when along came a little garden snake. It rustled the leaves beside me, and I jumped up so quickly in fear that I almost fell over the edge of the cliff. Thankfully, my friend grabbed me and steadied me, and I'm here to tell the tale of the wildly scary and not-at-all dangerous snake in the grass that was about 30 cm long (12 inches) and 1 cm (1/2 inch) in diameter. And let me tell you – snakes are a fear you have to come to terms with quickly when you choose to stay in Thailand for over five years.

My internal fears were:

Fear of people thinking I'm ugly.

Fear of people thinking I'm stupid.

Fear of people thinking I'm not good enough.

Fear of looking stupid in front of people.

Fear of looking stupid specifically when trying to speak a foreign language and screwing it up.

Fear of telling a joke that nobody laughed at.

Fear of people seeing me be scared of any of my external fears.

Fear of not being liked.

Fear of being made fun of in front of others.

Fear of not having my love returned equally.

Fear of people lying to me.

Fear of disappointing my loved ones.

Fear of saying I was going to do something, and then people seeing me fail. (Note: I wasn't afraid to fail ... only afraid to fail if people saw me fail.)

Fear of playing the piano in front of people in case I made a mistake, or they didn't think I was good.

Fear of really going for the ball in sports games in case I missed and looked stupid.

There might have been more (in fact I'm sure there was/is more) but I think you get the idea.

And I'm here to say that conquering those external fears is far easier than conquering those internal fears. But either way, conquering fears is exactly what I was doing out there in Asia.

Conquering My Fears in Southeast Asia

The moment that I announced my plan to travel so extensively, I was already facing the fear of disappointing my loved ones.

Looking back at my parents who were waving emphatically, tears running down their cheeks, and (fake?) smiles plastered on their face as I walked toward the security room, waving back and watching them disappear out of sight as I turned the corner. Part of me wanted to run back. I didn't want them to be sad, hurting, or missing me. I had a fear of disappointing them by leaving. I continued on because I knew that I needed to go on this journey for myself, and even to be a better daughter and support in the end.

✓ Two minutes into the journey, and already knocking down the fear that was keeping me living a life to please others

Early in the trip when I was visiting Alix in Paris, she had to go meet some colleagues for the day, and I spent the day wandering the city alone. It's Paris, which means this in and of itself isn't scary, and rather a dream for most people, however my fear lay in speaking the language which I'd spent about eight years studying but never had the opportunity to speak it. I walked into the bakery, and I said *"Je voudrais un café et un pain au chocolat, s'il vous plaît."* The barista nodded and gave me my order. She told me the price. I mixed up the numbers and gave her too much. With a smile, she handed the difference back to me, and off I went.

✓ Realized that making a mistake in a language didn't kill me after all. And it was better to speak and be understood somewhat, than to stay silent and out of the conversation.

After arriving in Chiang Mai, Thailand for the first time, we hiked into the jungle as a group. I have never considered myself an overly athletic person (despite the 8 km runs I did daily before leaving) and as we climbed up baby mountain, then mama mountain, then papa mountain in the middle of monsoon season, all I could imagine was tripping or sliding in the mud and falling. I hated this part. And yet, I knew that on the other side was a little village where we would meet a local hill tribe family and spend the night. The jungle was full of tarantulas, snakes, and I didn't want to know what else. And all I kept thinking of was tripping and falling. I was scared. And yet I kept going. And then I tripped, and I fell. And I tumbled head over heels down the hill, until I arrived I full-stop on my butt, shins bleeding, confused AF, and yet this laughter erupted from within me. I fell, and I was okay!

✓ I was hiking, scared of the heights, scared of the spiders and snakes, and scared of falling. But not only did I fall and not die – people laughed and laughed at how funny it all looked. They laughed AT me, and I also didn't die. In fact, I joined right in. I wished only that I could have seen the hilarious head over heels tumble in the mud as red and thick as clay.

About six months after landing in Chiang Mai the second time, I was invited to a friend's house in Mae Hong Son province because he was becoming a monk. And when someone becomes a monk a celebration by the family is had. So off I went with my friends to this celebration where his mother, his aunts, and his grandmas were cooking a Northern Thai feast like I had never seen before.

I. Ate. Everything.

And then?

I had to poop. Immediately.

And the only place I could do this was in a small bathroom with a squatter toilet, which you then pour buckets of water in to flush the stuff away. I was terrified. I didn't want to go. There was no electricity in the bathroom, so I had to bring a flashlight. I stood there thinking about it in fear. It was less than a year ago that I'd pooped in a public toilet back at home with a full toilet and seat, electricity, and flushing capacity. I remember standing there hoping the feeling would pass, and my friend said to me, "Kandis, are you okay?" I had gone pale as a ghost, sweat running down my face. There was no denying it at this point, the feeling was not going to pass, and I had to face my fear and use the bathroom. I grabbed the flashlight and held it in my mouth as I opened the door. And I'll tell you right now, it was a wild experience! My first-ever poop in a squatter toilet did not go well. I won't go into details, but I was in there about 20 minutes fixing the situation. I was sweaty, tired, and wet when I emerged, and everyone said "Umm, are you okay? You were in there for a long time, and you don't look so good!" I nodded. "I'm good!" And walked over to my friend, looked her in the eye, and said, "Oh man ... what a time."

> ✓ Fear of pooping in a public bathroom increased by 10 because it was a squatter after eating way too much spicy Northern food CONQUERED because while it wasn't amazing, I didn't die. And nobody cared about what actually went on in there, but just that I was okay. That felt nice.

And with that lovely story, I will end the conquering of the fears despite the fact that there are many more examples. I went ziplining high up in the trees, I spent more time in the jungle, I was on a tiny boat in a massive storm and convinced we would capsize, I got sick and caught my purse on fire in Vietnam (meaning no money, no debit cards), I lived in a city where I knew none of the language, I rode a motorbike, and almost got run over after falling off a motorbike. The list goes on.

But in the end, what I learned was that the only thing I really ever had to fear, was fear itself. In fact, fear is nothing but a thought in your mind that can either pass quickly or stick around creating this sense of fear – it just depends on how long you choose to hold on to it. When you step up and look your fears in the eye, they're far less scarier than you imagined them to be. And you're much stronger than you thought you were.

The Theories Behind Chapter 4

> **fear**
>
> /'fir/
>
> *noun*
>
> an unpleasant emotion caused by the belief that someone or something is dangerous, likely to cause pain, or a threat.
>
> —Source: dictionary.com

Many humans spend the majority of their lives paralyzed in fear and keeping it disguised by simply 'doing their job' or 'living a normal life'. On the outside they're going to work, having a family, attending social gatherings, and perhaps going on vacation once a year. But on the inside they have dreams and desires that they say no to each and every day because of the fear they feel when they think about what it would look like if they actually pursued these things. And so they keep on keepin' on, nothing changing year after year.

Because why?

Because fear.

And yet, fear is nothing but an emotion. An emotion that erupts when a thought pops up in your mind that's based in a belief that something 'dangerous' or 'bad' could happen in the future. And of course, a belief as we now know is nothing more than a story that we've created in our mind that we have chosen at some point in our lifetime to believe as a truth.

Take my own personal experience as an example. I used to be incredibly scared of heights and around the age of twenty-one, I was in a massive 4-storey mall in Toronto. I was looking over the balcony from the third floor straight down to the first to admire the Swarovski decorated Christmas tree that stood tall and towering and glistening through several stories. It was absolutely stunning. And when I was finished gawking at its beauty, I turned to leave the railing and became paralyzed in fear. I could not take a step away from the railing. It seemed impossible. The thoughts in my head were saying, 'If you step away, you won't be supported, the floor could crumble, and you'll fall to your death.' Meanwhile, there were tons of people all around me casually wandering the mall, looking over the balcony railing and then continuing on their way as if nothing was scary, strange, or difficult about this task at all.

And yet, I couldn't move. I was shaking and starting to sweat.

Logically, I knew that the floor was safe. Logically, I knew that if the third floor did go crumbling down, holding onto the railing wouldn't do me any good. And yet there I stood, frozen in place, gripping the railing like a life preserver from a capsized ship. All because a thought popped up in my head that if I took a step, I was going to fall and die, and my mind locked onto it.

I couldn't bear the thought of calling out to a stranger to 'help me' get away from the railing, but what was a girl to do? I was about to call out when suddenly I had another thought pop up that said, 'If you *crawl* away from the railing, you'll be fine.'

And so that's what I did.

In the middle of one of Toronto's most famous and busiest malls, I slid down to my hands and knees and crawled away from the railing toward the center wall yelling 'Excuse me! Excuse me!' to prevent people from tripping over me as I navigated the walkway at knee level. People stared, people pointed, but I didn't care. I just had to get to 'safety'.

I hope you're finding some humor in this, because I sure am. I'm literally chuckling to myself as I write this. However, at the time of course, I found it wildly terrifying and embarrassing.

The mall was (and is) a perfectly sound structure. And yet, one fleeting thought had me crawling around on the floor in a panic. Logically, I'm not sure what crawling did for me as far as the structure of the building and its ability to withstand my movement – but in the moment it's what my mind chose to believe. And it used to do this type of thing to me frequently when it came to heights. Thankfully, as I've practiced meditation and quieting the mind over the last decade, I can now take back most of that control when I hear these thoughts come into my mind. Because they still do. Perhaps I died by falling in a past life? I'm not sure where the thoughts come from, but they still arise when I'm on bridges, railings, or cliffs. But for the majority of them now, I can create a new thought instead. Because I can take back the control over my fear. I just have to flip my thoughts.

Fear is a Construct of the Mind

Think about something you're afraid of.

Go ahead, put the book down if you need a minute and think of something you're afraid of.

Anything.

Got it?

You sure?

Great.

Let me ask you ... is that thing that you're afraid of happening RIGHT NOW?

No. It's not.

Because if that thing was happening to you right now, I'm sure you wouldn't just sit there and continue to read this book thinking, 'Oh wow. Look at everybody laughing at me for failing at that project. I'll just sit here and continue reading.' Or 'My spouse is literally handing me divorce papers as we speak, but I really gotta finish the rest of this chapter.'

I mean look, I realize that this book is phenomenal and you don't want to put it down. But if your greatest fears were being actualized in this moment, no matter how good this book is you would most definitely have put it down by now.

Which means ... whatever it is that you fear is something that hasn't yet happened, OR it's something that has happened in the past and the memory of it is causing you to fear that it might happen again now or in the future..

Do you fear losing your job? That means you currently haven't lost it yet, because then you couldn't fear losing it. So you're thinking about and fearing something that hasn't happened yet. And it might never happen.

Do you fear that you're not a good mom, and your kids are gonna be screwed up, and it'll be all your fault? Well then they're obviously still young, or you couldn't fear that they'll grow up a certain way because otherwise they would be grown up already and you'd know how they turned out!

Or perhaps you see that your kids *have* screwed up in their life, and you fear that the way they are is your fault. This time you're fearing the results of something that has happened in the past and is no longer in your control. AND for extra icing on the cake, what you actually fear is still something that you have no control over in the future.

Making sense?

I've also seen people scared of driving in a car after a bad accident. "I had a bad accident, which is why I'm scared to drive now." Cool! Totally valid. However, this fear is caused by reliving a past event in the mind and worrying about whether it will happen again in the future. And of course, there's no way to tell if it will. Statistically speaking, (unless you're just a really crappy driver and don't pay attention to anything ever) the chances of you being in *another* accident are far less than the odds of you getting in the first accident, because most people don't even get in *one*. Making sense? Let's say the chances of being in a really bad car accident in your lifetime are one in a million. Then what are the chances of being in two really bad car accidents in your lifetime? Of course, it's far, far less. Maybe one in two million or one in three million.

So now the fear of driving isn't only a fear over something that may or may not ever happen (car accident) but it's a fear of something that is statistically improbable. And yet, the person may allow this fear they feel when they relive the accident in their mind to stop them from driving in the future, which of course has many ripple effects on their life.

So you see, any way you slice fear, it's not tangible, and it's not something that's happening to you right now, at this moment.

So then where is the fear coming from?

Fear Is A Story You Create

The fear is in the story that you're making up with thoughts in your head!

Or in other words, you're fearing your own thoughts and ideas!

We are so quick to create thoughts in our mind that turn into complete visualized stories with terrible outcomes that we don't even have time to realize that it's not real. That it's not happening.

An imagined possible outcome that may or may not happen in the future causes us to experience the emotion of fear.

Fear Example 1:

I was coaching an entrepreneur. She was telling me how she knew that the number one thing that would drive her business forward was to show up consistently on social media. So when I asked her why she wasn't showing up consistently on social media, she replied, "Because I'm scared."

"What specifically are you scared of?" I asked.

"I'm scared," she said, with a deep sigh and a pause, "that if I show up frequently, I might get kidnapped."

"Wow," I said. "So this whole time you've been shying away from showing up publicly in your business because you're scared you're going to get kidnapped?"

"Yes," she replied. "And also, I'm afraid that people will think that I don't have anything valuable to say."

"Aha," I replied. "First things first. How many people do you see showing up on social media every day *without* getting kidnapped?"

"Millions" she said.

"Right, so the chances of you being kidnapped are slim to none. Especially if you don't advertise your address, right?"

She laughed, and said "Yes, you're right."

"Okay great," I said. "So the second point is that you fear that you have nothing valuable to speak of. What happens if people *do* think that?"

"Well," she said, thinking deeply, "I guess, nothing really. They don't buy from me."

"Exactly. And are people buying from you now?" I asked.

"No," she said laughing again.

"Great. So, either you show up on social media and *maybe* someone buys, or you don't show up on social media and *definitely* no one buys," I said. "The real question then is, when are you showing up on social media?"

"Today," she said.

And she did.

She showed up on social media five times that week and nothing bad happened at all. In fact, good things happened. She received engagement from her followers, and most importantly – she realized that she was 100% capable of showing up in her business, and that the thing she feared wasn't nearly as scary as she made it out to be. She was overthinking it and building it up with stories and thoughts in her mind.

Fear Example 2:

I was working with another client specifically on mindset and achieving calm and peace of mind. She was a self-proclaimed catastrophizer (one of the mind traps we go over inside my program, which identifies the most common afflictions of the mind). She was telling me this story about how one day her husband was coming home from a late work meeting, and he said he'd call before he left the office. But it was getting late, and she hadn't heard from him.

She called his phone but it went to voicemail. She started to worry, pacing around the house, wondering what might have happened to him. He's now an hour late, and still not answering his phone. She started to panic and called one of her friends in tears, sobbing that she was concerned that he'd gotten in an accident on the way home. And so she started calling the local hospitals to see if there had been any accidents.

Nobody seemed to know where he was, and she was full of anxiety, on the verge of a massive panic attack when he walked in the door apologizing for being so late. He had got caught up with a client, and his phone was dead. His extra charger for the car was still in the overnight bag from their weekend getaway a few days before. She was so overwhelmed, the tears continued to stream down her face, and she hugged him as tightly as she possibly could.

Turns out, he was completely fine. All that worry, panic, and shedding of tears was for no reason.

***

In Example 1, this digital entrepreneur wasn't moving forward in her business because a thought popped into her mind that maybe nobody would buy from her. And by doing nothing at all, she was actualizing her biggest fear that nobody would buy from her, because she wasn't even making her offer visible and marketing herself!

In Example 2, this woman worked herself into a panic attack based on one fleeting thought, 'what if he's had a terrible accident?' There was no evidence to support that other than the fact that he hadn't called. And yet, the fear took over and panic ensued.

My Three-Year Struggle With Anxiety and Panic Attacks

During my first month in Thailand, I was with my travel group on a boat for a full-day snorkeling excursion off the coast of one the southern islands. Suddenly a storm blew in and our captain let us know we had to turn back and head to shore quickly. The boat was being tossed around in the water and our entire group was huddled in the main galley way to help steady the boat. The kayaks we'd been towing got caught in the undercurrent and the force with which they were pulled under was enough to rip the railing they'd been tied to clear off the boat. I could see at least five people in my periphery who were puking off the side of the boat, and I was glancing around the boat to find the lifejackets – of which I could see about eight - for all thirty people.

The thoughts that began to arise in my mind were of panic. I believed in that moment that I was going to die. I took hold of my great-grandmother's necklace, which I wore around my neck and began silently praying to her and my other deceased grandparents to *please* help me. I was terrified. And then I felt something very strange starting to rise up in my body. I looked at the guy who was sitting next to me, and I said, 'I don't feel well'. He told me to look at the coastline to help me feel less queasy. 'No, I'm not queasy,' I said. 'It's something else.' He told me I didn't look so well and to lie down on the bench, but I couldn't lift my legs. They were no longer under my command. My mind told them to move, but they barely flinched. And so instead I hurled myself off the bench onto the floor.

The rest of that boat ride was kind of a blur. We had three nurses on our boat who were taking my vital signs while others brought me blankets or anything else to cover me with in case I'd gone into shock. When I finally started to feel okay, we were docked at the marina and most people had already left the ship. I got up weak, exhausted, and completely terrified of what just happened to me, and my friends helped me off the ship. The medical center wasn't open, but I called Dr. Penny – my doctor back home – and told her what had happened. Turns out I had a stress-induced seizure. In other words, a very intense panic attack.

She told me I'd be okay, to rest up, drink lots of water, and take care of myself.

But from that day forward, I was living in constant fear of it happening again. I joked with friends saying, 'It's great to know that when I'm in danger my body just chooses to shut down – thanks a lot!' But deep down the idea of that terrified me. And so any time I got some jitters from coffee, or felt groggy from a sleepless night, I would start to think, 'Oh no! It's happening again!' And then I'd spend the next hour or sometimes two drowning in thoughts and visualizations and stories about what *might* happen.

I couldn't focus, sometimes I'd just start crying, and it was wildly uncomfortable. There were several times where I would go to the grocery store, put everything in my basket, and then while I was waiting in line to pay, the anxiety would hit me like a ton of bricks, and I'd just put the basket down and leave the store. I was terrified most of the day. Every time I'd have a random shake or a twitch in my body, my mind would say, 'You're gonna die!'

Then one day, after years of this getting progressively worse, I was sitting on a restaurant patio with my parents for dinner. They were talking, and I was nodding, but inside I was losing my mind. Every noise, every flicker of light in the corner of my eye, every time someone passed me, I would think my body was going to fail me. My nervous system had been running on high for so long, it was just shot. Everything made me so anxious. And then someone dropped some cutlery, and it was the tipping point. I jumped out of my chair, tears streaming down my face and asked my mom to follow me to the parking lot. I paced back and forth, sobbing. I still remember her face watching me, the sadness of not being able to 'fix it' for me. I finally crouched down on the pavement and said, 'If this is what life is like, I don't want to live it! I need help!' And then I stood up and leaned into my mom for a massive hug as I cried my eyes out.

The next day, I called a therapist. I went to a couple of sessions, and we had some good discussions, but it soon became obvious that what she was telling me was 'just mindfulness'. She said to me on my third appointment, 'Kandis, you're welcome to continue coming to see me. But with the mindfulness tools you have, I really don't think there's anything else I can offer. You know and under-stand all the tools of mindfulness, you're just not applying them to yourself in this situation.'

And a light bulb went on that day.

It was all in my head! All this anxiety and fear was created by me! By my own thoughts!

I began trying to challenge my thoughts instead of allowing them to overcome me. And it was very difficult. I still had a lot of fear, and one day soon after this meeting, I was so worried about the possibility of having a panic attack that I actually sent myself into a panic attack. And so I walked back and forth and back and forth outside of this café in Koh Chang where it happened, and so many people stopped to help me, to get me water, and to make sure I was okay. And I just had to keep walking. It felt like every single muscle in my body was constricted and my mind was racing faster than I ever thought possible. It felt awful, and I just kept walking back and forth, focusing on my breath and the movements of my legs until it finally dissipated after about 15–20 minutes.

And then I started laughing.

I thought, 'I'd rather experience that once a week than experience the fear I've been gripped by 24/7 each day.' The *fear* was the most painful part of the entire thing! Panic attacks don't actually kill you, and so I realized I'd been spending most of my days consumed by fear of something that was simply uncomfortable for 15–20 minutes.

From that day forward, when I had the thought, 'It's happening again!' I'd reply back 'And so what if it does? It doesn't last very long.' And then the temptress of fear in my mind would respond, 'But what if you die?' and I would say, 'Well, then I die! But I'm not going to live in fear of it 24/7!'

And *slowly but surely* I flipped the thoughts, and no longer have panic attacks or constant anxiety.

Anxiety is fear. And fear is created by a thought in the mind.

When we challenge the thought, we free ourselves from fear.

Fear vs. Danger

In all of the above scenarios, fear is present but danger is not.

It's incredibly important to note the difference between fear and danger. Danger is real and it's happening in the present moment. Fear is created in the mind.

For example, I can now confidently walk up to a railing in the mall and look over. Then if that illogical fear thought pops up, which it sometimes does, I have trained my brain to respond with, 'Nope, this is not logical. Simply step away, Kandis. Look around. You're fine.'

On the other hand, when I was about twenty-four years old, I met a stranger on a late night bus on my way home. He was sitting next to me, and we got to talking. Eventually we found out that he lived in my same building! So we got off at the bus stop and walked to the building together. Turns out that he actually lived in another city, and I ended up locked in my own apartment as he attempted to rapc me.

Personally, I don't think there's room for fear when you're actually in danger.

My fight or flight response was in high gear, and I was acting on autopilot. I ran to the apartment door and he blocked it. Then without any conscious thought I ran out onto my balcony and started screaming my apartment number and for someone to call 911. My attacker felt fear of being caught, and he turned to leave my apartment. He opened the door, and then pointing to the apartment number on the door he said, "Don't worry. I'll be back." and slammed the door on his way out.

I ran to the door and locked it. I slid down the wall and then my mind started racing. Conscious thought had returned.

"What if he comes back?"

"What if he had blocked the balcony door too?"

"What if I hadn't been able to get away? What else might he have done?"

The fear kicked in when I finally had time for thoughts. When in imminent danger, most people report not really knowing how they got themselves out of it – they just *did it.*

Like the time in Chiang Mai when I was driving my motorbike and I was cut off by a pick-up truck. One moment I was driving my motorbike and saw the pick-up truck in front of me. The next moment I was standing next to the truck, and my motorbike was laying underneath the truck, one of my wheels wedged under one of the truck wheels. In a split second, I somehow managed to jump off the bike, throw it down, and end up standing there in the middle of the road, not a scratch on me.

The driver got out and helped me get my bike from under the truck. It wasn't damaged and so I hopped back on and started driving away. A few yards down the road I had to pull over. I had started sobbing so badly I couldn't see where I was going, and I was now shaking with fear, adrenaline coursing through my body. The thoughts racing through my mind were, "Oh my god! How did that happen? I almost died!" Once again, when the danger was over and conscious thought kicked back in – so did the fear.

And yet ... so many of us humans live our lives in this fear. We're hardly ever actually faced with the danger we daydream about – and yet we live in fear that maybe we might be someday possibly.

The Modern Human Life of Fear

My friend and fellow coach Mark Bailey and I were talking one day about just how much of our modern human life is lived in fear. And he made an analogy that I love.

We're a part of nature, but we don't really act like it.

Because real nature is always living in the present moment. An example I like to give is that gazelles are on the African plains and they go out there and eat their food, but there are lions out there too that eat the gazelles. Yet the gazelles don't wake up in the morning and say, 'Omg guys, are we gonna go out there today? There are lions out there that might eat us!' Instead, they just get out there, eat their food, live their day, and they're in the present moment. Then the only reason they're actually scared or have some sort of fear is when they actually see the lion. THEN they'll respond and react to it. They have to have clear and present danger right there in front of them before they react to it. But humans? No, we bring clear and present danger – that proverbial lion – with us throughout the day. And so even though 99.9% of the time that lion isn't going to eat us, we think it is, and that stops us from doing things.

Key Takeaway

Danger is real. When you're experiencing it, it's happening in the present moment. Fear, on the other hand, is created by our thoughts about what *might* happen possibly someday sometime in the possible future. And so I invite you to flip those thoughts. Stop letting them have so much power over you.

Just like I did when I was experiencing my anxiety, challenge those thoughts of fear. If what you're imagining *does* happen, then what? You can deal with it when/if it happens rather than allowing it to steal your presence

> *Danger is real ... it's happening in the present moment. Fear ... is created by our thoughts about what might happen.*

and peace of mind for days, weeks, months or years. Because remember ... almost always, the fear of something happening is far scarier than if that something actually happened.

CHAPTER 5

Learning to Become My Own BFF

I SAT THERE CROSSING my arms in front of my chest so the other kids couldn't see the Mickey Mouse print I had on the front of my t-shirt. It was 1995, and I was sitting at my desk in homeroom wondering when the teacher was going to finally enter the classroom to temporarily pause the laughing, pointing, and taunting I received each day from the other students in my class. Today, the focus was on my Mickey Mouse t-shirt, but it didn't really matter – I could have worn the trendiest clothes around and they simply would have found something else to ridicule me for.

The "Bully Girl" as I shall refer to her, sat in the middle of it all, a smirk on her face, enjoying the control she had over everyone who put me down.

It hadn't even been a full year since Bully Girl and I were actually friends at our elementary school. We were the only two students in the grade who lived on the other side of the school district line, and so when everyone we'd gone to school with for the past six years went to one school for junior high, we were sent to another. At first, I was actually excited to start Grade 7 in a new school. In my mind, I imagined meeting new people and having new experiences. I chopped my once waist-length hair into a shoulder length bob, my 'baby fat' was finally taking a hike, and despite the expected nervousness, I felt genuinely excited about my new adventure at a new school.

And it started off great. Together, Bully Girl and I made a lot of friends. We were invited to lots of sleepovers and birthday parties, but Bully Girl had a very strict, single mom who rarely allowed Bully Girl to join us. Instead, she spent most of her evenings and weekends babysitting her little sister while I was out having fun with our new group of friends. To this day, I can only guess that it was jealousy that caused her to suddenly decide to make my life hell, but whatever it was – she was out for me with a sudden vengeance, quickly getting the rest of the class to gang up on me and tease me about every possible thing they could find.

One day, one of our previously mutual friends came up to me at my locker and pretended to be having trouble getting into the locker next to mine. "I'm sorry we're so mean to you," she said quietly with her head down. "She's making us. I'm sorry," she repeated and walked away quickly as if not to get caught.

Each day it seemed to get worse. Bully Girl sat there in the middle, laughing and pointing at me, encouraging others to make jokes. At first the others would look away from me, or look sideways, but eventually they'd laugh and chime in.

Some days it was my clothing. Other days it was my hair, the way I sat, or how I doodled on my notebook. I'd try to shrink down in my chair as if I didn't care, or as though I couldn't hear them.

I remember the last day I ever voluntarily raised my hand to answer a question in class. On that particular day, I was called upon, I gave my answer, and all I could hear was laughter and snickering.

"Listen to her voice," someone said.

"She sounds like a man," said another.

"Why does she even talk?" someone asked.

I could feel my face burning red with shame. I wanted to disappear. And I never raised my hand again until college. If the teacher called on me, I'd mumble "I dunno" and put my head down.

At lunchtime they would throw things at me and make fun of me for what I brought for lunch.

The lunch breaks became so unbearable that eventually my mom started picking me up to go home for lunch every day. I'm so freakin' lucky that my mom was able and willing to provide me with a safe haven for an hour each day at lunch. I would race out the door where my mom was waiting in the parking lot at the first bell, and if we arrived back to the school early, we'd sit in the car until the bell rang again so I didn't have to spend even two minutes more in that school than I had to.

I am still thankful every day for that escape. I know other kids who never had that. And I'm also incredibly thankful that social media didn't exist back then. Evenings and weekends, I would hang out with my friends from my previous school and pretend that Bully Girl and those other people didn't even exist.

Words Can Leave Scars

The following year, we gave the school board my aunt's address so I could switch schools and be with all my old friends.

Having my friends around me for Grade 8 was so much better, but I'd also put on a lot of weight during that traumatic year. I still got bullied, but not as much — snide comments that I was fat, that I would never get a boyfriend. At least I had a group of friends who would build me up and be there for me, but I still did what I could to hide in the shadows. The less the people at school noticed me, the better it was. Although like most bullied kids, I would day-dream of waking up one day gorgeous and popular and getting all the attention from the boys.

It was the summer between Grade 10 and Grade 11 that I started eating about 300 calories a day and working out for 2–3 hours at the YMCA. I was so sick and tired of hiding, of being called fat and ugly, that I was willing to do whatever I needed to change my body. (*Note: I do not in any way recommend this. It's very dangerous and actually sets you up for more weight gain in the future.*) I would tell my parents that I was eating dinner at my friend's house, and then when I got to my friend's house, I would tell them I'd already eaten at home with my parents. I ate a bagel every morning, and some-times an apple in the afternoon. If my friends put chips out, I'd have one or two when they were looking, but it made me feel sick.

I had created a belief that I was worthless if I was overweight. And in order to be liked or worthy of love or attention, I had to be thin and pretty.

And sure enough, when I got back to school that September, my belief was reinforced to me when the guy who used to bully me the most in high school walked right up to me and said "Wow, Kandis! Lookin' good!"

He stopped right in front of me as I walked into the school, and we stood there, face to face.

"There's a party this weekend…" he continued, looking me up and down, "do you want to go with me?"

I stood there for another minute, still saying nothing. All I could think was that this is what I'd wanted, wasn't it? To be liked and worthy? To get attention from the boys and the popular kids? Part of me wanted to say yes and go to the party and hang out with the cool kids. And the other part of me wanted to punch this kid in the face. Couldn't he see it had been the same ME this whole time? But instead, I said "No, I can't," quietly under my breath and started walking away.

He yelled after me, "Come on Candy Cane, come to the party with me!"

And surprising myself as much as I did him, I spun around, flipped him the middle finger, and yelled "Or you could go f*** yourself!" before spinning backward on my heels and continuing down the hallway to my next class with a huge smile on my face, and my entire body shaking with anxiety.

Becoming 'Cool' and Popular

When I started college three years later, there wasn't even one person I'd gone to high school with on the whole campus. With all these new faces I noticed quickly that I was catching the attention of the boys. Suddenly it felt like all the boys in the class were interested in getting to know me, and the girls were eager to befriend me.

'Holy crap! I think I'm cool!' I thought to my self.

I was acing my classes, I was the life of the parties, I was grabbing up boys left right and center, and it felt amazing. I was cool, and popular, and everyone knew who I was. (At least – that's the story I was telling myself.)

And deep down I was terrified that it would all come crashing down. I was terrified that one day I'd arrive at school and they'd all turn on me just like they did in Grade 7. And so instead, I turned on them. I started putting other people down, making fun of them in front of others.

It seems like such a cliché, doesn't it? The bullied becomes the bully.

But my ego was trying to keep me safe from the pain it once felt. It was finding a way to not have to experience that again.

I was mean to my classmates. I'd sleep with guys just for the sake of showing people I could. I'd flirt with the guys that I knew other girls liked, just to show them that I had the upper hand. I wanted to show them that I could have them at any moment if I wanted them.

And that behavior didn't stop when I left college.

I had to be the girl that could cut the line at any nightclub. I had to be the girl who never had to pay admission to the hottest parties. I had to be the girl that danced with the guy all the girls were drooling over. And I had to be the girl that other girls were afraid to approach, and who could, with one nasty (or flirtatious) look, get any person in the club to buy me drinks, give me their seat, their spot in the lineup, or anything else I desired.

I was dating multiple people at once (if you could call seeing them once every four weeks dating) and I prided myself on their desire for more from me that I was unwilling to give. I used many of them for free drugs, or to get an invitation to the most exclusive parties.

And that's where you found me at the beginning of this book – looking like I had an awesome *Sex and the City* lifestyle on the outside and becoming more and more a shell of a human on the inside.

Because no amount of parties, sex, diet pills, designer clothes, or drugs can ever replace your own inner self-worth.

The drugs and alcohol were taking over my life, and just as many hours as I'd spend dressing up in the hippest clothes, staring at myself in the mirror, and taking photos by night, I'd spend curled up in disgust, unworthiness, and guilt the following day.

Because no amount of parties, sex, diet pills, designer clothes, or drugs, can ever replace your own inner self-worth.

Eventually, I knew things had to change.

Becoming Someone New

I stopped hanging out with my party friends and started hanging out with a new group of people I knew from a previous job. They had Sunday BBQs and Wednesday evening potlucks and game nights. They were incredible people, and I had a lot of fun. And I also wondered when the ball would drop. Would they turn on me? They never did turn on me, but I pulled away instead.

"Besides," I would tell myself, "I'm leaving for Thailand anyways. I don't have time to be making new friends."

I felt like things would be different when I left. I had this image of me in flowy hippy-style clothing, sun-kissed skin and hair, confident in my own skin, and not giving a f*** about what anybody thought of me.

I had this image so deeply ingrained in my mind that when I went shopping for clothes for the trip, I bought clothing that fit into the persona I'd created in my mind instead of who I truly was – black, pleather, skulls, darkness, and edginess. At that time, I didn't realize that I could be carefree and confident in any clothes.

Funny isn't it? I wanted so badly to be confident in who I was, that I bought clothes that resembled nothing of who I was. In my head, it was the hippy traveler that seemed most at peace in their skin, and so off I went with a suitcase of clothes to dress as the person I wanted to be.

Less than two weeks into my trip, I found myself in London, meeting up with an old friend. I realized that despite wearing the confident hippy clothes, I felt nothing like a confident hippy. And in the exclusive private nightclub my friend took me to, I longed for a little piece of my true self already – just a few weeks into my trip.

I felt so out of place, dressed up as someone I wanted to be rather than who I truly was. And that feeling followed me to Thailand a month later. The first day that I got to meet my travel group for the tour I'd signed up for, there was a group of girls I immediately labeled "cool". They were beautiful, super fit, and wearing fabulous clothes. All my insecurities washed over me like I was drowning in the ocean.

From the moment I saw those girls, I immediately thought, *They're not going to like me.* And so I kept my distance. I was short with them when they talked to me because I was suddenly self-conscious of everything I was going to say. Back home when I'd felt like a VIP, I had my posse of people around me. I had the bouncers, bartenders, and DJs to prove I was cool. I had the designer clothes and stunning outfits to prove I was beautiful, and a group of gorgeous people by my side to prove that I was enough.

And now here I was, on the streets of Bangkok in a burgundy cotton tank top, denim shorts, and a macrame belt, no makeup on my sweaty face, and my short hair flying out in the most random curls brought on by the humidity, feeling exposed, unworthy, and ugly. I no longer had my mask to hold up in front of me, my army of support at my side, and the material items to show everyone I'd made it.

It was just me.

Feeling naked, exposed, and alone.

I Needed My Best Friend

In that moment I wished so badly that I hadn't left my best friend Alix, who I'd been hanging out with just a week ago. With the support of my best friend beside me in Paris, I'd been wild, confident, and the life of the party. And yet here I was being quiet and feeling small.

I did make friends in the coming days with many other people in the group, and I had an amazing 40 days hopping the islands in the south of Thailand. But that feeling in that moment stuck with me, and it was then that I knew I had to change something inside of me.

Just like that story I wrote that day at Thai 1 On Bar, "*And when these layers are stripped away to reveal your most intimate characteristics, you have to ask yourself – 'Do you like what you see? Are you who you thought you were?'*"

I didn't like what I saw actually. I didn't want to feel wild, free, and confident only at the side of my best friends, or when I was dressed in the most fashionable clothing. I wanted to feel that way all the freakin' time. And to do that, I realized that I needed to *become my own damn best friend*. I knew that to have that confidence and freedom of the hippy-clothes-wearing woman in my imagination, I needed to believe in myself without the posse, without the clothes, without the bouncers, bartenders, and DJs to build me up.

The hurt and pain I felt growing up feeling sorry for who I was, well, it had to go.

I had been hiding myself for far too long, leaning on people and things to prove my worthiness, and it was time to let myself be free. Be free to be who I am and be free to be the incredible person I knew I was capable of being.

And I tell you this entire story, starting back when I was just a child, because when people see me now, in front of a crowd, I'm the outgoing, confident, edgy person working the room and making friends. I'm the one quietly introducing myself to the person sitting on the side who's looking lonely and uncomfortable, introducing them to new people, making them feel as comfortable as I possibly can. I'm the one wearing ripped jeans, skull necklaces, a unicorn backpack, and a partly shaved head.

You know, just the other day I found myself in a video Zoom call with five amazing friends, (I'm looking at you Dana, Katie, Kimi, Chrissy and Amber) and we spent 90 minutes going in a circle complimenting each person one by one, telling them exactly what we admire and love about them. And when it came to me, the general theme was that they saw me as someone who acts boldly, holds herself with confidence, and isn't afraid to be herself. They said they see me as someone who truly knows who she is, who isn't afraid to show that person to the world, and who loves herself deeply, which exudes that confidence and boldness.

Hearing them say this filled me with joy. I felt seen in that moment, like all my hard work learning to love myself had finally paid off.

I AM that don't give a fuck what anyone thinks hippy girl – just sub skulls and pleather for the flowing hippy-esque clothes.

No More Hiding!

I'm not hiding anymore.

I live this life knowing that I have no guarantee of another one. And I don't want to live one more second of it trying to be someone I'm not, trying to dim my light, or *not* doing things because it will make others uncomfortable. I'm over that.

I love who I am now. I am 100% my very own best friend. And when I have my very own best friend with me at all times, I'm able to be that bolder, brighter version of myself anywhere I go.

For just a moment, close your eyes and imagine that you've just walked into a room of 200 people. You're alone, and you don't know a single person in that room. How do you feel?

Now imagine once again that you've walked into that same room of 200 people you don't know, but this time you've got your best friend with you.

Do you feel that surge of confidence you get knowing you have them by your side? That's the same surge of confidence I get knowing that I have *me* by my side. When you become your own best friend, your own personal cheerleader, therapist, and your own personal support system ... when you truly dig deep into who you are, discover your worst and best characteristics, and change what you can and honor what you can't ... When you know yourself that well, a deep love for yourself can open up. And with that deep love, the doors to the magical places outside your comfort zone can also open up.

And so I tell you this story of how I was treated, and how far I've come, because I want you to know that the way that I am is *learned*. Even as a two-year-old, I hid behind my mom's legs when someone came to the door. Over the last decade, I have taught myself to truly, deeply love myself. I have taught myself to be kind, compassionate, and loving toward myself.

You can teach yourself the same, and I hope you do.
Because when we do that, the possibilities for us in this life truly become limitless.

The Theories Behind Chapter 5

Are You Your Own Friend? Or Foe?

You've probably heard the saying that we are our own worst critic. But I find it more accurate to say that we are often our own worst enemy. When we take a deep look at the way we talk to and treat ourselves, it's often horrific. Just imagine if we spoke to our friends the way most of us speak to ourselves. Chances are, you wouldn't have many friends left.

In 2013, I flew home from Thailand for my cousin's wedding, and I was in the car with my parents. We'd just loaded up the car with our overnight bags and began the drive up to Blue Mountains for my cousin's wedding. We hadn't even gotten but two minutes up the road when my dad says, *"F***! I forgot my pills!"*

I don't remember if it was me or my mom who said, "Well good thing we haven't gone too far! Let's go get them!"

And my dad continued, "F*** I'm such an idiot! I can't believe I did that! I *hate* myself!"

And my mom and I just burst out laughing. "Wow, Dad!" I said, "That's pretty intense! You hate yourself because you forgot your pills? AND we're literally right around the corner from the house?"

We couldn't believe what we were seeing. My dad was fuming.

We turned around, got the pills, and then started once again on our journey. This time, after we'd been driving for about 10 minutes, I yelled out, "I forgot something!"

He slowed the car and asked if it was important. I said it was, and he calmly took a deep breath and said, "Okay, I'll turn around up here, and we can go back."

I started laughing and told him I was only kidding. He called me a stinkerbutt, and we continued our drive.

But do you notice the difference between his two responses? When I, his sweet darling daughter, forgot something he was very calm and really quite pleasant about it. However, when he was the one who forgot something, he completely lost it on himself — even going so far as to say he hated himself.

And this is a common occurrence. Most people are a lot harsher towards themselves than they are to others. And yet …

From the moment you're born, to the moment you die, there is only one person who will be with you always. Every other person in your life will come and go. Some will stay for long periods, and some for short. But no matter what, there will always be one person (and one person only) who remains by your side from the very beginning to the very end. And that person is you. And so I ask you … how's that relationship going?

For most of the people I work with, the relationship with their own self is one of the worst relationships they have in their life.

For example, just imagine that the reactions above were reversed. Imagine I told my dad I forgot my pills and he starts swearing, saying "You're such an idiot! How could you do that? I hate you!"

I probably would have jumped out of that car in a puddle of tears, picking up the pieces of my broken heart on the way out.

All too often we have no trouble saying nasty, harsh things to our own self that we would never dream of saying to another person

– especially one we love. So why do we say it to ourselves? Do you think it actually hurts any less when *we* say it versus when someone else says it?

We have no trouble saying nasty, harsh things to our own self that we would never dream of saying to another person – especially one we love. So why do we say it to ourselves?

I want you to stop for a moment and think of something you might have said to yourself recently that you would never dream of saying to a good friend or someone you care about. Have you told yourself that you're not good enough for someone or something? That you're too ugly, too fat, too thin, too tall, too short, too white, too black, too weak and/or too stupid to do something or to connect with someone? Have you ever thought your hair's too thin, you have too many wrinkles, you have nothing interesting or of value to say, or that you're not funny enough to make new friends, meet a partner, or have any type of awesome relationship? Have you told yourself you're not as smart as other people? That you're not good at something you love? Do you compare yourself to others and always feel like you just don't quite measure up?

Do you catch yourself saying things like, "What's wrong with you?" or "UGH, I can't believe you did that again" or "Why would you say that?" or "You're so stupid!" on the regular?

If you said yes to any of those things above, then that means … you're human!

We all get wrapped up in these thoughts at some point. And while it is normal, the goal is to experience them as *infrequently* as possible, because these thoughts have some pretty negative effects on us and our lives.

The Brain's Reaction to Negative Self-Talk

Whether we are saying negative shit to ourselves, or someone else is saying it to us, our brain considers it an attack. In other words, our brain can't tell if we are making the attack on ourselves, or if it's someone else attacking, and we're in danger. And of course, it fires up the ol' fight/flight/freeze response.

There's a quote by Carl R. Rogers that goes,

> *"The curious paradox is that when I accept myself just as I am, then I can change."*

I love this quote because it illustrates how if we are constantly berating ourselves and getting angry at ourselves, saying negative things to ourselves, we don't actually change for the positive. Or at least, it's much more difficult to do so.

Our brain isn't as clever as we like to think it is. In fact, we are much more clever than our brain.

Read that again.

We are much more clever than our brain.

It's important to remember that our brain is simply a tool that we use to help us stay alive, rather than us actually *being* our brain. We can outsmart our brain with positive reward systems. And part of that is self-compassion. When we constantly berate ourselves for being too fat, too skinny, too stupid, too slow, too this or too that, we are putting ourselves into fight or flight response, which creates more cortisol and adrenaline in the body which in turn shuts down parts of the prefrontal cortex which helps us make logical decisions, and keeps us from experiencing joy, true happiness, ease and flow in our lives.

Guilt, shame, and anger toward oneself all produce this similar response.

I used to work for a global addiction rehab facility based out of Thailand as their content creation and digital media manager. During that time, I learned a lot about addiction and how it works within the brain. And one of the things I found most interesting was the cycle of shame and guilt. For example, many people would say drug, alcohol, or food addicts should 'just stop consuming'. And I see where that's coming from, I really do. It seems like the logical thing to do, right? However, it's not that simple.

Chemicals such as dopamine do come into play, but also guilt and shame.

Let's say we're talking about a food addict. This person binges out on junk food the night before, and then wakes up in the morning feeling fat, ugly, and really guilty or ashamed about their behavior the previous night. They try to shake it off and get ready for the day, but as they shower and get dressed, they look at themselves in the mirror and think, "You stupid, ugly pig. Look how fat you are. Why can't you just control yourself?" They vow never to give in to their cravings again. But at the same time as they say this to themselves in the mirror, their body is perceiving it as an attack and/or a punishment. This increases the body's energy into the FFF response, and once again decreases the energy being sent to the pre-frontal cortex. Which of course we're now learning is responsible for logical thinking, problem solving, and controlled emotional response. Their negative emotions intensify, and their body immediately looks for a hit of dopamine (the 'feel good' hormone), which is derived from food (or any drug or alcohol). Now ... the logical response, especially based on what they just said to themself in the mirror would be to say NO to the food. However, their logical center of the brain doesn't have as much energy or power because they've just been 'under attack' by their very own thoughts. And thus, their ability to make powerful, logical decisions is decreased. So, they eat the food for the instant gratification it provides, and then they get even more mad at themselves a moment later. And so the cycle continues.

And this is why we must be as kind to ourselves as possible ... so that we are triggered into the FFF response only when true danger or stress is around. And the less we talk down to ourselves, and the more we practice pride, gratitude, and love toward ourselves, the more our body and brain can relax, and our logical processing centers can stay fully online. Not to say you'll never feel anger, get triggered, or be upset again – but it will happen with less intensity.

You'll also have moments when, for example, you'll strongly disagree with something. You'll still have the thought, your body's physiological response just won't follow suit – or to such an extreme extent.

You can still have a debate, or have strong opinions, feel sadness, hurt, or pain, but the goal is that your FFF response doesn't fire up at just the slightest hint of any of these things.

Being kind to yourself is more powerful than most people realize.

Because it helps calm our nervous system.

Self-Care vs. Self-Compassion

In recent years, I've noticed an influx in #selfcare posts, and people talking about how important it is to take time for yourself no matter how busy your life is with work, kids, etc. Take that bath, go out for dinner with your friends, spend time reading a book, or go for a hike in the outdoors. I've seen posts that self-care is about bath bombs and music in the tub, or self-care is drinking wine or beer with good friends. Whatever it is, I love the concept.

However, none of that matters if your mind is being bombarded with worry, guilt, anxiety, and negative self-talk the entire time. It will be wildly more valuable when you combine self-care with self-compassion.

The problem is, of course, that many people don't even realize that these are two different things. That is, they *could* be one in the same, but in these modern times they're more often not.

Self-care typically leans toward working out, going for walks, spending time alone, or perhaps quality time with someone you care about. Self-care could be manicures and massages or brunching with your friends. It could be playing sports or taking time off work.

But none of that will really benefit you if you're not being kind to yourself while you're doing it.

I've watched so many people I care about take some well-needed time off for 'self-care' and then spend the whole time berating themselves in their mind for not working and wasting their time.

I've seen many women especially choose to take some time for themselves and go out with their girlfriends, only to end up in tears (or near to it) because they don't know what to wear that doesn't make them feel too fat or too ugly to go out in public.

Speak to yourself with compassion like you would your own best friend.

I've seen people too scared to spend a night alone because they're afraid of how nasty their own thoughts can be.

When it comes to self-care, the most important areas to focus on is how compassionate you are toward yourself in your own thoughts. To speak to yourself with compassion like you would your own best friend.

Sympathy, Empathy, and Compassion

I had the opportunity to learn from Thupten Jinpa, the principal English translator for the Dalai Lama, at a conference one year. The way he described compassion – and specifically self-compassion – stuck with me. He said:

> *Sympathy* is when you feel pity towards someone for something negative that has happened to them.
>
> *Empathy* is when you feel and understand the pain someone is experiencing when something negative has happened to them.
>
> *Compassion* is when you not just understand what the person is feeling, but you take it one step further and wish to offer your assistance or a helping hand.

For example, imagine your friend has just lost their job. With sympathy you might say, 'Sorry to hear that. I know how much that sucks."

With empathy you might say, "I feel your pain, as I've been there before. I'm sorry that happened to you, it's not easy."

And with compassion you might say, "I understand this must be so difficult for you. What can I do to help you at this time? How can I support you?"

And so, similarly, when it comes to *self*-compassion, you're responding in a compassionate way to your own feelings, thoughts, and life struggles. When my dad left his pills at home on the way to the wedding, he reacted in anger toward himself, but he reacted with compassion to me. If he'd acted with self-compassion, he would have reacted the same way to himself that he did to me – with kindness and willingness to help resolve or better the situation.

> *"Self-compassion involves the capacity to comfort and soothe ourselves, and to motivate ourselves with encouragement when we suffer, fail, or feel inadequate."* —Chris Germer

> *"Compassion is an underlying human emotion that creates great positive physiological change, because we must have compassion, especially for our offspring, or we wouldn't survive as a species. And so we are compassionate beings, and our physiology changes for the better."* —Dr. James Doty

> *"You are the only person in your life who will be with you from the moment you're born to the moment you die. Everyone else will come and go. Some for long periods, and some for short. But you are the only one that is constant. So, make sure that relationship is a good one."* —Kandis James

The Importance of Self-Compassion

Being self-compassionate is the biggest step toward becoming your own best friend. It's really about learning to treat yourself as kindly as you would a friend or loved one. You'd never look over at your friend and say, "Wow, you're so fat. That shirt looks terrible on you, I can't believe you even wore that out." And you definitely wouldn't follow that up with, "What's even more unbelievable is that you don't have any clothes that look better on you because you have zero willpower to control yourself and you keep eating garbage and getting fatter. What's wrong with you?"

You wouldn't walk up to a friend/coworker and say, "I can't believe you made that typo on page six of your report – you don't deserve your position here at this office. In fact, I don't even know why they hired you in the first place."

I mean, maybe you might say these things, but I doubt you'd keep many friends.

And yet, if you're like most people, you say things like this to yourself all the time.

And so just like we discussed flipping our thoughts when it comes to fear, we can do the same when it comes to how we speak to our own self.

I invite you to take notice in which areas of your life you are speaking to yourself in a negative way. How can you flip those thoughts to positive ones to create a healthier mental state and overall better life for yourself?

> *"Every negative thought we have, especially directed toward ourselves, is like laying a brick. One or many bricks are laid each day until you're in a self-made prison with no light. And you can only ever get out if you first know that you're inside."*
> —Dr. James Doty

Effects of Self-Compassion

Not only does being self-compassionate feel good and help us attain our dreams, it also offers the following amazing benefits:

- Decreased chance of depression, anxiety, and stress (aka improved mental health)

- Increased ability to be happy, resilient, and optimistic (aka HECK YEAH!)

- Release of oxytocin (aka 'cuddle chemical' or 'love hormone') in the body, which increases relaxation, trust, and psychological stability
- Decreased cortisol levels (aka your stress hormone)
- Increased confidence
- Better relationships with others

Exercise: Be Your Own BFF

It's one thing to understand the concept of self-compassion, and an entirely different thing to practice it. I'm inviting you now to take a moment and put down this book. Take a couple of deep breaths and close your eyes. Then take a few minutes to think about all the 'not so nice' things you've said to yourself in the last few hours, days, or weeks and write them down on a piece of paper.

Take as much time as you need and think of as many things as you possibly can.

If you're having trouble thinking about these things in this moment, take notice of the thoughts that arise over the next few days. Keep a notebook with you and jot down any nasty thoughts you say to yourself and then come back and do the second part of the exercise when you've got that list.

Once you've got your list of 'not so nice' things you've been saying to yourself, I'll invite you to take a new piece of paper and for each and every negative thing you said about yourself, write something nice to combat that on this new piece of paper.

It might make it easier to imagine that your best friend is the one who said the negative comment about themself. Then

---

think about what you might say to them if you heard them say that. How would you respond? How would you offer them some compassion?

For example, if one of the things you say about yourself is 'I'm too fat'. You could write on this new piece of paper, 'My weight doesn't equal my worth. No matter my size, I'm a kind and good-hearted person.'

Once you've written at least one positive response for each 'not so nice' thing you'd' written down, tear up the sheet that had the negative comments, and keep the positive ones for any time you need a reminder!

Key Takeaway

What it boils down to is that all too often we put our happiness, strength, and confidence on other people. We spend all of or most of our energy trying to make others happy, building *them* up, and encouraging them to live *their* best life ... all the while being the harshest to our own selves. And then we wonder why we don't succeed in the way we want to. We wonder why our relationships are suffering, and why we feel anxious and down on a regular basis.

And all of that can be changed when we make a conscious decision to become our own damn best friend. When you love yourself as much as you love your best friend, and treat yourself with compassion instead of negativity, you'll be amazed at what becomes possible for you in your life.

> *Make a conscious decision to become our own damn best friend.*

CHAPTER 6

Let Your Intuition Guide you

SHE HANDED ME a notebook and I looked down at the cover. There was a printed graphic of what appeared to be small shops, and a strange looking dog among some hills. The text read "You are so beautiful to me ~ we are want to made landfall on the coast of Ireland ..."

I burst out laughing.

My friend Asia who had handed me the notebook burst out laughing too.

She and I met five years before when we both first arrived in Thailand and decided to make a life in Chiang Mai. In the years that followed, she became one of the closest friends I've ever had. She also knew how much I loved Thai stationary with wildly incorrect English translations on the cover. Laughing, I read it out loud again for both of our enjoyment as I opened the front cover and the laughter quickly turned to tears.

Inside the notebook Asia had taped photos of me and all my friends in Chiang Mai, and then had each one of them write me a note or sign their names by their photos. As I flipped through the pages of memories and well wishes, the tears turned to full-out sobbing from both me and Asia as we sat across from each other at a small wooden table outside the restaurant across from the airport. My plane was departing in just a couple of hours, and I had no idea when I would return to the Land of Smiles. All I knew was that when I did return, it would be as a tourist, not a resident.

I hugged Asia so tightly it's a surprise one of our heads didn't pop off. I was standing in front of her and yet I missed her already. For the past five years she was there for me always. She understood what it felt like to have two homes. That while I was in Thailand I talked about Canada as home, and while I was in Canada I talked about Thailand as home. No matter where I was, I missed the people closest to me. And here I was, about to hop on a plane, and close one of the most enlightening chapters of my life.

Not wanting to scare off the other patrons with our sobs, we said our 'see ya later's' and I walked through the doors of the airport leaving the thick, humid air behind me, not knowing when I would feel its embrace again. I looked back and saw Asia driving off on her motorbike, her thick curly hair waving in the wind, and a tear streamed down my face as I thought about how long it might be before I saw that sight again; a sight that had become almost a daily occurrence over the last five years.

Beginning New Chapters

I checked my bags and made my way into the waiting area for my flight where I opened the book again and began flipping through the pages. I read all the messages my amazing friends had left for me and remembered each of the moments captured in the photographs. It was my own decision to leave the country, and yet here I was, a heavy ball in my chest as tears continued to stream silently down my cheeks, interrupted only by small bouts of laughter and smiles as I read the silly messages inside the book.

I closed the notebook and it signified something even greater than what it appeared – it signified a new chapter in my life.

And I smiled.

Yes, I was crying here in the airport as I waited to depart the country I called home for so many years. Yes, I was going to miss my friends. I was going to miss the food, the ease of life, and of course the weather. I was going to miss the sense of oneness that I felt in that city that I'd never felt anywhere else before. I have loved cities and countries that I've travelled to. I've enjoyed my time there. But with Thailand, and specifically Chiang Mai, it was as though the moment I set foot on that ground I felt like I had come home. I felt like I belonged there, that I'd finally returned to where I was meant to be after so many years of flailing around lost. This beautiful place with its beautiful people and its beautiful energy, helped shape me in so many ways into who I am today in just a few years. And I was *also* ready for the next step.

It was like my time in Chiang Mai, and my time spent travelling the world, was setting me up to be the person I needed to be to achieve what I wanted in this life. And what I've always wanted was to help other people. But it's true what they say … you must fill your own cup before you offer it to others. And that time I spent away was exactly what I needed to peel back the layers of my own being and emerge a stronger, healthier, wiser version of myself.

I was ready to go home and start changing the world. I was ready to find a way to show others that life can be everything you've hoped it could be. I was ready to show people that when you decide to take control of your life, everything and anything becomes possible.

But in true fashion, the universe knew I had more lessons to learn before I was truly ready for my mission.

And that lesson began about two months before I left Thailand.

A Bold and Beautiful Lesson from the Universe

The sound of waves crashing, people talking and laughing, and terrible electro music filled the air as I sat at a small wooden table at Nature Beach Resort's restaurant. My fingers were dancing rapidly across the keys of my laptop as I knocked out the final copy for a client's website. I just needed to finish a few more pages before my one-month vacation on Koh Chang, an island in the south of Thailand, would officially begin. My friend Amy was arriving tomorrow, and I wanted to be completely done with this project by the time she arrived.

It was then that I heard the sound of someone chatting to a staff member and being seated at a table nearby. And as he sat, he laughed a deep, honest, and contagious laugh. I glanced over, and there he was, this man with his long dark hair, intense tan, and 'don't give a fuck what you think' attitude. I'd barely had a chance to comprehend what I was seeing in that moment, but it took my breath away just the same.

He was good looking, yes, but that's not what took my breath away. His energy pulled at me like nothing I'd ever experienced before. I had a deep pull inside of me telling me that I had to get to know this human. I was being pulled toward him, not physically of course, but energetically. The whole while he sat there and ate his pasta, he was completely oblivious to this energetic hold he had over me.

I so desperately wanted to go over and talk to him, and yet simultaneously I felt that I would puke from nerves if I actually attempted it. And so I sat there, completely distracted, attempting to continue writing until he finally finished his pasta, paid his bill, and left.

I watched him go, and thought, "F*ck, now what?"

I thought about following him, but my nerves told me it would be better to stay put. So instead I ordered a pina colada and dove back into my work.

The following day when my friend Amy arrived, I told her about this guy I'd seen and how he made me feel. She laughed at me for not introducing myself. She laughed because, she said, I am one of the boldest people she'd ever met.

She and I met in Chiang Mai a couple years prior when she was traveling through the city for *Songkran,* the name for Thai New Year. We became instant friends and remain so to this day, despite never having lived in the same continent.

The day of her arrival on Koh Chang, we sat by the beach having cocktails, playing cards, and generally catching up about life. We went back to the room, got ready for dinner and walked to a nearby place on the road toward the main strip of town where the nightlife was. And so we sat there eating and drinking as one does, and guess who shows up and is eating at the same restaurant? Obviously, I'm talking about *that* guy!

I was beside myself as he sat there eating. Amy kept telling me to go over and say something, but I felt frozen in my chair. Eventually he was finished and was about to leave on his motorbike when I panicked and whistled louder than I ever knew I could. He looked up, making direct eye contact with me across the open-air restaurant. I think I was as surprised by my whistle as he was, and now it felt like it was someone else who'd taken charge of my body and was waving him over toward our table. He paused for a moment in consideration, but then began walking over, and I noticed that my whole body was shaking. I'd never felt so nervous to talk to a human in my life. And the first thing he told me was how rude I was for whistling at him.

I'm laughing now, thinking about this hilarious interaction, because I don't even recognize who I was in that moment. But I apologized to him for any offense and told him that I'd just wanted to speak to him. We talked for a few minutes, and he said he'd be at the Banana Leaf Bar if I wanted to talk more later. Of course, when Amy and I finished our dinner we went directly to Banana Leaf. And there he was, sitting at the bar on his own, talking with the bartender. He invited us to sit down, and he and I got on like wildfire. The laughter was non-stop, and his energy continued to pull me in.

When Amy left a week later, he and I spent every single day together. It felt like a magnet was holding us together. I adored being in his presence, and he would answer the questions I was thinking in my mind before I even spoke them out loud.

As it turned out, we both had flights out of Bangkok booked for the same day. We said our goodbyes, but he left first. And when he was in the airport, he sent me a video message telling me that he really thinks we have something special, and he hoped we could see each other again. But of course, no pressure.

My entire being leapt with joy when I watched that video, and I ended up going to see him on my way home from Thailand. And so that day when I was leaving the airport with tears streaming down my face, there was a sense of sorrow for what I was leaving behind, but there was also a sense of joy for new beginnings. I had a mission to accomplish when I got back home, but first I had to learn more about this mysterious human who was drawing me in like nothing I'd ever experienced. So, I flew to France to visit my friend Alix for two weeks, and then arrived in Italy to see Pablo.

We laughed until we cried, we stayed out dancing until 5 a.m., we made homemade pasta, spent afternoons in the garden, and spent nights lying under the stars and talking until the wee hours. My three-week stay quickly turned into five, but it still felt like a flash before I was back home in Canada visiting my aunt and uncle's cottage in Northern Ontario for the weekend.

The Soulful Decision-Making Process

We sat outside the quaint, beautiful cottage on the large deck off the back of the kitchen that overlooks a deep blue lake with white stone shores. We were lounging in the sun, enjoying our snacks and Prosecco when my uncle asked me what I had planned now that I was back in Canada for good.

"Actually," I said with a grin, "I'm leaving at the end of the summer to go to Italy for a couple months."

He couldn't hide the shock on his face. "But I thought you were moving home!" he exclaimed.

"I was!" I replied, "But, things have changed, and I'm going to spend some time in Italy with Pablo."

I remember him nodding his head as he took in this information. I felt like I knew what he must have been thinking; my parents had been so supportive of my being away, but they missed me like crazy. And they'd been so excited for my return. And now I was leaving?

He nodded and asked me, "How do you make your decisions? This is a big decision, and it changed so suddenly. I'd love to know how you make your decisions."

I sat there for a minute, contemplating his question. I'd never been asked this before.

Eventually I said, "Well, I guess you usually have two options, right?"

And I put out my two hands on either side of me, face up.

"Option 1", I said as I raised my right hand up, "and Option 2," I said, as I raised the other hand.

"I guess I just think about Option 1 fully," I continued. "I allow myself to daydream and imagine in as much detail as possible what Option 1 would look like if I chose it. I create almost a mini movie based on where my imagination goes when I think about that option. And once I have a really clear picture, I notice how that feels within my body. As I imagine this option, I ask myself 'How does my body feel? Good? Calm? Excited? Anxious? Scared? How does it feel?' And then I move on to the second option and do the same thing. Then, whichever one feels better within, I go with that one!"

"Hm, interesting," he said, "very interesting."

And then our conversation moved forward to another topic. But I remember that conversation so vividly because it was the first time I actually verbalized how I make life's biggest decisions, and I realized that I was making decisions in an entirely new way. I wasn't writing pros and cons lists like I did when I was younger. I had become so in tune with myself that I didn't need the logic aspect, I simply needed to understand the feelings of each option.

And that's how I made the decision to go spend more time in Italy with Pablo. Every part of my being was telling me to choose that option. And so I did. And what he taught me was more valuable than anything I ever could have tried to learn in a course or through any type of program.

Amore Italiano

That trip was the beginning of a two-year long distance relationship that forced me to learn about myself and who I was in entirely new ways. Pablo challenged my thoughts, and pushed me to be a more mindful, aware human being. But in the beginning, I took his actions and words to mean that he wasn't being nice. Just like traveling on my own, being with someone who had such an overwhelming sense of who they were and what they wanted out of life was a whole new experience. This man knew who he was, and if I or anything else didn't complement his lifestyle, he wasn't interested.

What I failed to understand for so long was that he was the embodiment of that person I saw in my mind that I had wanted to be – that person who is so fully themselves that they won't invite anything into their life that doesn't make it better. And he loved me. He loved me deeply, and I loved him back. And he was also brutally honest, and I had a hard time accepting that then.

He didn't sugar coat things; he didn't tell me things just because he knew I wanted to hear them. He spoke only his truth. He challenged my ideas and beliefs. He challenged who I thought I was. And while I was stronger than I'd ever been, I wasn't yet strong enough to not see these things as a personal attack. And my inability to see what he said as *his truth* vs. an attack on me was causing problems in our relationship.

When we first got together, neither of us wanted anything serious.

We were both traveling a lot, I'd just broken up with my fiancé a few months before, and I was moving back to Canada. We both agreed to keep it light, easy, and fun. However, after coming to see him that first time, we agreed to a committed long-distance relationship. I spent much of my time going to Italy, or once we met in Thailand for two months on the beaches of Koh Chang where we first met. But as eighteen months of a long-distance relationship approached, I was starting to feel annoyed with spending months at a time in Italy, away from my own home. I wanted to focus on my business. I wanted to make money, create an impact, and finish my courses in mindfulness meditation at the university.

The story I was creating for my own future had begun to change from the one I'd painted when he and I first got together. I look back now and see that without consulting him, I had created a vision of how I wanted our future together to be, and suddenly I wasn't willing to accept anything else. I wanted him to want the exact same things as I did, and I was furious with him when he didn't. I had changed and expected him to change too.

Of course, this started to cause arguments between us, and our laughter wasn't as deep and it didn't come as often. One day, almost two years into our relationship, I was spending Christmas in Italy with him. It was Christmas Eve of 2017. We were at this beautiful restaurant in the basement of an ancient stone building in the square of Perugia, and we had just been served our second course of an incredible eight-course meal when I looked at him and I said, "This just isn't working, is it? I love you so much. And we're going in two different directions right now. When I look at you, I get angry, and I don't want that. Because I love who you are. So, I think I need to change my flight and go home in January instead of February. What do you think?"

He looked at me, the sadness in his eyes mirroring mine, and he said, "Yeah, that's okay with me."

He brushed a tear away from my eye, and then we had the most beautiful night. The laughter and lightness returned, and as we left the restaurant, we kissed in front of the fountain in the square, a most romantic scene for any couple, but especially a couple who had just broken up.

You Don't Always Get What You Expect ... But Perhaps It's Better

When I first felt the pull of his energy that day by the beach, I thought the universe was showing me my soulmate, my life partner. But with him, the universe delivered something possibly even greater – the lessons and growth I needed to become the person I needed to be in order to create the future that I dreamed of. My time spent with Pablo taught me things about myself I may never have come to terms with on my own, or it would have taken me years longer to discover.

Two months before that Christmas Eve dinner, I was in Canada finishing up my schooling for the specialized applications of mindfulness at the University of Toronto. We were having a conversation over the phone that got particularly heated. I was very angry with him, in fact getting quite heated in my words. And he said to me, "If this is the way you're behaving, then you'd better go back to class, because I don't think you're learning what you're supposed to."

I remember feeling the hot surge of anger flood my body. "How could he say that to me?" I roared internally. I was furious with him. Who did he think he was?

But I laugh now looking back because he was right. I was getting far too caught up in my emotions and taking things personally. I wasn't letting things flow, and instead I was becoming attached to expectations that I had created out of thin air in my mind. I was understanding the *theory* of what I was learning about mindfulness, but he helped me understand what it

Which means that we are all literally and truly interconnected.

looked like to put it into practice in the most difficult situations. It just took me a little while to realize that.

We remain good friends to this day, he and I. But the year following that Christmas Eve was one of the hardest years of my life. Everything he'd consciously or unconsciously taught me in that time together was finally becoming abundantly clear, and I was growing rapidly, becoming a more evolved and wiser human with each and every insight I received as I reflected on our time together. Just like in the original Grinch movie where they show his heart growing three sizes that day, I could see myself growing faster than I'd ever grown before.

And I also cried a lot that year.

Writing this chapter, I cried a lot too. I sent a text to my darling friend and Inner Voice coach Dana saying, 'I'm realizing why I was

Sometimes growth is painful. And it's always worth it.

resisting writing this chapter for so long. I guess I'm still continuously healing. And with that, continuously growing, expanding, and getting stronger."

Because for me to share these moments with you, I must put myself back in these moments as vividly as possible. And the moments

I spoke about in this chapter were freakin' difficult for me to get through. But it's these moments in life that feel difficult, the moments where we're at a crossroads, the moments that feel like screaming *WTF?* ... these are the moments that teach us how to move forward. It is in these moments that we are shown what life is truly about. Because when we feel these things, we're on the precipice of change. Of transformation. And change, despite what many think, is not scary, but exhilarating. That is, IF you trust yourself enough to know that you're on the right path.

The Theories Behind Chapter 6

When my uncle asked me that day how I make my decisions, it was the first time I'd ever really thought about it and tried to put it into words. Since then, I've realized that the way I make decisions is not necessarily the norm. Rather than simply tuning into how it 'feels', you'll often notice that people revert to logic, reasoning, and pros and cons lists when it comes to the decision-making process.

And I'm not here to knock logic or reason. I run my own business and I've been working in digital marketing for close to a decade. I absolutely understand the need for logic, numbers, and problem solving when I'm making plans – or roadmaps as we call them inside my online program *Live Your Dreams* – to get us from point A to point B in life or in business. When it comes to the specific details, things like logic, reasoning and list-making are extremely valuable tools. But when it comes to making decisions about life's big picture, I always look toward my inner feelings, or my gut response.

Two Brains – Gut and Head

Have you ever had a gut feeling that something was wrong? Or that something was right?

Have you ever felt like you knew something so deeply despite no logical reason for knowing this?

For example, someone says something to you and you automatically get tingles in your stomach and you think, 'They're lying.' Or you enter into a room and think, 'Something isn't right here', only to find a few minutes later something goes wrong.

We once believed that neurons – the special cells in our body that are responsible for transmitting messages from our brain to our body – only resided in the brain, which was inside the head. But more recently we've discovered that we have over 100 million neurons in our gut. So those butterflies in your stomach? That uneasiness you feel when something is happening? This is what many researchers are calling our second brain.

Our body is designed to be able to receive messages in more ways than one. However, we live in a society where our education systems rarely focus on helping us tune into these ulterior methods of receiving information and making decisions. Modern schools teach children how to use logic, reasoning, and problem solving while most of the time completely disregarding the gut feeling, or what some people might call intuition.

---

in·tu·i·tion
/ˌint(y)o͞oˈiSH(ə)n/
noun

the ability to understand something immediately, without the need for conscious reasoning.

—Source: dictionary.com

Without conscious reasoning we often know far more than a lot of us like to give ourselves credit for. And when we learn to really tap into our intuition and start to notice how frequently it's 'right', or how frequently it guides us in a positive direction, then the more apt we are to use it and rely on it in the future.

When I was a kid, my parents and I would go to a sports bar, and they had this trivia game on the TV. We each had our own electronic device the restaurant would give us where we could input our name and then choose our answers from the multiple choice questions on the TV screen. As a young kid, my parents were surprised at how often I was getting answers right. And my method was this: when I had no idea what the answer was I would simply 'feel' the correct answer. I would get out of my logical brain, stare at the screen, and one of the multiple choice answers would start to appear brighter. And that's the one I would choose.

I noticed that if I allowed my logical brain to come in and second guess what I saw or felt about the correct answer, the chances of me being incorrect would greatly increase. And when I could fully detach that part of my brain and lean into those feelings and just 'see the brightness', I tended to do quite well.

Now I understand that's not exactly a controlled science experiment that could be considered proof of intuition, but it's still pretty cool, right!? Here's an eight-year-old in a pub testing out her own theories on intuition. I was always so amazed at how well I could do when I was able to turn off that logical part of my brain and just choose the multiple choice answer based on which one 'felt right'.

And clearly, I still use that method as an adult – except instead of trivia questions, I make all major life decisions based on these feelings. And I do my best to remember to make my daily decisions this way as well.

Tapping Into the Universal Energy

Remember in Chapter 2 when I said that the universe is always speaking to us and it's our job to listen? I'm not talking necessarily about big impossible-to-miss signs like a strike of lightning. Humans are energetic beings. We are made of atoms; we are literally made of energy. And our energy feels and responds to outside energy sources from the rest of the universe.

I had the pleasure of hearing Dr. Dan Siegel speak at the A Mindful Society conference back in May 2019 and what he said can really help us understand our interconnectedness and human ability on a greater level.

He spoke that day about micro and macro states and quantum physics. It was fascinating and also a little bit complicated. I'm going to do my best to give you the completely simplified Kandis Notes version of what really stood out to me.

A science experiment was done whereby they separated two photons from their single source and placed them maybe one meter (three feet) away from each other. When scientists moved or manipulated one photon, the second photon would show the exact same change. So they decided to move them farther apart. Many miles apart, when one of the photons was moved or manipulated, it stayed true that the second photon would show the exact same change.

Combined with quantum entanglement theory (look it up if you're keen to learn more), it suggests that the electromagnetic forces that exist within all living things on this planet are quite literally connected. Which means that when we examine the Big Bang Theory (no, not the show) everything that currently exists was once part of one energetic hot spot that has since been expanding. Which means, of course, that we are all literally interconnected balls of energy stemming from this one original source.[3]

By understanding that we have all been formed from the same original energy mass, we can understand that feeling or being affected by another's energy is not woo-woo, hippy-dippy, or airy-fairy hooplah.

It's science!

It's real!

---

3   If you're interested in learning more about this, I recommend reading *Aware* by Dr. Dan Siegel.

We are essentially balls of energy moving around this Earth, and we're connected energetically to every other energetic being on this planet. Which is why making decisions and moving through life using only the brain that you have inside your skull is limiting your potential. When you rely solely on logic and theory, you're not tapping into the infinite wisdom and energy of the universe that is constantly guiding you and supporting you through life.

That is, if you let it.

In order to truly let the universe guide you to the lessons you need to learn, or to the greatest possibilities and success in your life, you've got to stop operating from those limiting beliefs and stories that are cutting you off from this universal guidance and preventing you from aligning with the energetic frequencies of joy, success, and abundance.

Energetic Frequencies and Vibrations

Everything, including humans, is made up of energy, and energy is made of up frequencies. And just like a radio antennae, our bodies are constantly and unconsciously tapping into the energy of all that is around us.

You've likely seen a meme or a t-shirt that says "Good Vibes Only" – it's talking specifically about energetic vibrations or frequencies. Our bodies can pick up on the energetic frequencies being put out by people, situations, thoughts, ideas, things, or places. Different moods send out different energy waves or frequencies, which is responsible for how well you 'vibe with' people or places at any given time.

For example, imagine that you're super tired and feeling run down, and all you want to do is grab some food and head home to rest. You walk into a restaurant to get some takeout and they're blasting electro dance music from the speakers while you wait for your food. You might find yourself instantly irritated. In fact, depending just how tired you are, you might not even place your order, but rather walk out and decide to order delivery when you get home.

Now let's imagine instead that you just found out that you got the promotion at work you'd been hoping for. You're super excited and can't wait to get some takeout and go home to celebrate. You walk into that same restaurant, and it's blaring that same music from the speakers, but this time you find yourself dancing to the music while you wait instead.

In the first scenario, the energy that you were giving off based on your lack of energy overall did not meet the energy of the music. In the second, you were excited about something that happened, and the energy of your excitement matched that higher energy frequency from the dance music.

Music as an Illustration of Energy

Music in general is probably the easiest way to illustrate this energetic connection. How often does someone say, "What do you *feel* like listening to?" when they're putting on music? Or "What are you in the mood for?" Inadvertently, we're inquiring as to what energy frequency will best suit your own frequency at that moment. So just like we can choose our music based on our current energy level, we can also use music to *change* our energetic frequency and improve our mood!

Big events like Tony Robbins are constantly playing really high energy songs during the breaks and even sometimes during the main event to get people hyped up and excited. Before an interview or something you had to do in your life that you felt nervous about, did you ever put on your favorite song to ease your nerves and get you 'ready' for what you had to do?

Music is an easy way to see and understand these frequencies. But these connections go far deeper than that.

If you are constantly stewing in negative thoughts, it's going to bring your own vibrational frequency down. And because similar frequencies find each other, you're going to find yourself in an external reality that continues to draw more of that negativity into your life. Not only will you *see* evidence based on your own thought perception – which as we know is based on your past experiences, your physical and emotional state, and your learned morals, ideas, and beliefs – but you can also attract positive or negative things based on the energetic frequency you're putting out into the universe.

So those negative thoughts you've got on repeat inside your head? They're *really* not helping you in this thing we call life.

Self-compassion Can Raise Your Vibration

Just like negative thoughts on repeat can lower our vibration and attract more of the same – when we stay in a positive thought space, we can raise our vibration and attract more positivity instead.

When we think something negative or positive, our body not only hears it and reacts to the words, but it can feel the vibrations with which it is said.

Say the following statements out loud or in your head and notice your body feels differently with each one:

'You are an amazing person, and I hope you get everything you desire in life.'

'You are worthless, and you'll never be good at anything in this life.'

Did you notice your own energy shift as you read those sentences? Perhaps you felt a lightness and sense of joy with the first. And in the second perhaps you felt a heaviness appear in your chest, a physical impulse to move, or a fleeting emotion of sadness or self-doubt.

Now think back to what we discussed in the last chapter and how often you say something mean to yourself. Each time you say that, you're literally changing your energy vibrations.

In the documentary *I AM*, by Tom Shadyac, they show the results of 'The Rice Experiment'. You can find many people online who will attempt to prove this experiment doesn't work, but it's also been duplicated many times with the same results – even by regular people in their home.

And the experiment goes a little something like this: Two sterilized jars are filled with cooked rice. One jar is labeled something nice such as 'I love you', while the other is labeled with something such as 'I hate you.' Each jar is then placed within the same conditions (temperature, direct light exposure, etc.) but with some distance between them. Each day the 'I love you' rice is showered with compliments, love. And affection. The other jar is told hateful, mean comments instead. Over time, the 'I hate you' rice begins to grow mold and rot at a much quicker pace than the positive, 'I love you' jar of rice. In fact. In the experiment shown in *I AM*, the 'I love you' jar of rice looks relatively edible while the 'I hate you' jar is already black with mold.

Just imagine what your own negative thoughts could be doing to your body. And, imagine the type of low level energy we are putting out into the universe, which of course in turn we're attracting more of the same to us.

Lean Into Your Intuition and Universal Guidance

Sometimes the universe guides us in unexpected directions. Take for example, my meeting with Pablo. Sure, I had a romantic escapade and gained a lifelong friend, but even more so I got the lessons and experience I needed to evolve into who I needed to be for the next chapter of my life.

And it's important that we stay open. Try not to get too attached to what each of the universe's gifts will bring to you. It's easy to create stories in your head of how you think things should be, but we must remain open to seeing things as they are instead. Sometimes things will start later than you want them to or end sooner than you expect.

But simply lean into the wisdom.

Key Takeaway

Keep your vibration high with positive thoughts, and make your decisions based on whole body feelings. And when you are faced with saying goodbye to things you don't feel ready to say goodbye to, let there be a certain grace and joy in it because you know that when you let something go, you're making room for something more.

CHAPTER 7

Accepting Change and Letting Go

I COULDN'T BELIEVE THE grandiosity of the hotel as our cab pulled up to the main entrance. White and modern, grand and lit up like the White House, I marveled at the building as I hopped out of the car into the warm, humid night air while Jenna paid the driver. She joined me and we walked into the open-air hotel, across a marble tiled foyer, and back out the other side into a lush tropical garden with a restaurant lit up next to the sea.

It was April 2015 and my girlfriend and I were in Bali, Indonesia. We'd been there for about four nights already staying on another part of the island, but tonight Jenna said she was taking me out somewhere special. And special it seemed to be.

We approached the host stand and Jenna let them know we had reservations. As the staff chatted amongst themselves, I admired the decor of the restaurant, the joyful sounds of the patrons, and the smell of the delicious food wafting through the air.

"Right this way," said a man from behind us. We turned to face him and to my surprise he began leading us away from the restaurant I'd just been admiring. We started walking down a path through the garden and past the massive swimming pool. The farther we went, the more confused I got, but Jenna was ignoring my questioning looks and chatting with the host as we walked instead. And when we turned the corner around some immaculately groomed hedges, it all became clear.

Romance in Bali

In front of us was the beach, the waves crashing on the shore, and a pathway lit up with candles leading to a table on the beach. The table and chairs were adorned in white linen, candles and flowers filled the table, and large flags of white fabric blew in the breeze next to it. All the while the waves continued to crash against the dark night's shore in the background. It was something out of a fairytale. Or at least something from all the brochures I used to look at when I was a kid. I was overtaken with joy and felt like I could cry. In that moment I suddenly remembered that I'd told Jenna one night in passing how I'd always wanted a romantic dinner on the beach. And there we were in a most beautiful scene on a tropical beach in Bali. It was more than I could have ever imagined.

We were invited to sit down, our toes in the sand, and a bottle of wine on the table. Our host poured us each a glass, and we shared a toast to begin an incredible meal. A three-course meal of delicious seafood and local flavors was followed by dessert and champagne, and a wedding proposal. There on the sand, our tummies full of delicious food and wine, Jenna asked me to marry her. And I said yes.

We'd met in Chiang Mai several years before, but only began dating just over a year before. She'd already come to Canada and met my family, and I'd gone to South Africa to meet hers. That night on the beach we laughed, we cried, and we spent hours calling family and friends to tell them the news. And we spent the next six months planning a wedding that would take place in Chiang Mai. My whole family was going to come out to Thailand for the celebration, and it all seemed like a fairytale. We spent days looking at venues, scanning Pinterest for decoration ideas, and talking about where we'd live and how we'd spend our honeymoon. And yet, as the wedding came closer, our relationship seemed to float farther and farther away.

Letting Go of What is 'Supposed to Be'

Deep down I started to feel like this wasn't what we should be doing. And yet our families had been invited, I had a ring on my finger, and the house we were going to live in together was under construction.

Part of me felt like I should just power through and continue with our plan because that's what seemed easiest. And then another part of me was scared that doing that would only lead to more unhappiness. When I thought about ending things, all I could think about was the gorgeous wedding, having my whole family finally come visit me in this place I called home, and then our honeymoon, the incredible house we planned to live in, and our (at times) jetsetter lifestyle. She and I were even working on building a business together.

If we were to break up, all of that would be lost. Shattered. Gone.

And this is what is tough in this life isn't it? Everything has a ripple effect.

Part of me thought it would be easier to just continue on rather than dealing with splitting up a business and changing what I perceived to be my whole future.

And then one day I decided that I just had to accept my feelings and share them with her. I was honest with her about my fear of not being with a man again in my life, and my fear that we were living *her* lifestyle instead of mine, and my fear that we were simply moving too fast. And it turned into an argument that couldn't be resolved.

We talked about trying to make it work, but it became clear quite quickly that it would never be what it once was.

And so, with a heaviness in my heart, I called my family and told them the wedding was off – that there would be no epic family party in Thailand. Part of me still just wanted to power through. We had planned this amazing event, and it would have been so much fun. Part of me wanted to hold on to that dream that we created together. Part of me wanted to pretend that the arguments we were having weren't happening. Part of me wanted to pretend that we were happy.

Part of me thought that pretending was far easier than facing the truth of another 'failed' relationship, of having to call off a wedding, of finding a new place to live by myself, and otherwise facing the world all alone once again.

But I knew deep down that pretending would only be easier for the moment. I knew that keeping up that facade would only turn into anger, resentment, and sadness.

When Letting Go is Hard, But Hanging On is Worse

Which is why I made that decision to bring everything up when I did. I figured it would likely end things between Jenna and I, but it was better than sticking with something that didn't light me up.

We often get so caught up in how we think our life *should* go that we have difficulty accepting how it's *actually* going. We put on a fake smile and power through instead of facing the truth, which is usually far more difficult. But it's only more difficult in the beginning. Once you get through that initial discomfort and pain you realize you are free to do and be whatever you want, instead of faking your way through a situation that doesn't fill you with joy.

People fake happiness all the time because they're scared to own up to the truth. They're scared of what people will think when they say how they really feel. They're scared they won't fit in, people won't like them, that they'll lose some of what they have in life.

At the beginning of this book, I told you how I was doing exactly that! I was doing what was expected of me by society and the world, and I wasn't doing what I truly wanted. And I felt that I was crazy for being unhappy with all that I had in my life. But each and every day, a little piece of my true self was dying. I was getting further and further away from who I knew I was deep down inside. And thankfully, I was able to receive an awakening that turned my life around.

But that feeling of losing a piece of me each and every day was what was happening to me again in this relationship. It appeared sunshine and rainbows on the outside as she and I jetted around the world, hosted awesome parties, and generally enjoying life. But I didn't feel like I was living *my* intention in this world. Thankfully, I remembered that I wake up every morning to my own choices from the day before. And it was time to let go of what I thought would be and move forward once again on my own path.

The World is Constantly Changing

The world is constantly changing, and to expect us to stay exactly the same, staying happy and content always doing the exact same thing is, quite frankly, insane.

Inside my *Live Your Dreams* program, I help my clients get clear on what they truly want out of life. And so often they get caught up in this idea that we have *one* purpose in life. That we are supposed to find *the thing* that makes us happy. But what if it's not about that at all? What if it's about learning to ebb and flow with life, doing what makes you happy when it makes you happy and letting go of the idea that we ever need to choose one thing and hold on to it?

My students and clients often quickly realize once we start working together that what they *thought* they wanted my help with to create in their life, actually isn't the most important thing. We discover what *truly* makes them tick, rather than what they believe *should* make them tick. And every single time I watch a client go through these exercises and experience this transformation, it brings me to joyful tears.

We are bred by our society to believe we need to be a certain way and are often not aware of how much that affects us on a regular basis. To see those restrictions or regulations on life tossed away to reveal what we *truly* want for the first time … well, that's powerful.

My seven years abroad originally began as an idea to travel for 3–4 months so I could get the travelling 'out of my system' and focus on what I was supposed to focus on – creating a business or finding my career path.

But then I decided to tack on a year in Australia. The way some family and friends responded to the news, it almost felt like I'd confessed to murder. "You're doing what? At twenty-seven? What about your job? Your career? This is gonna set you back!"

But I knew what I had to do, and I pushed through.

And then funny enough, when I got to Australia, I didn't even like it. Yet instead of saying to myself, *'Well, you said you'd stay here for a year, you'd better do it! What will people think when they find out?'* I followed my heart and went back up to Chiang Mai instead. I then planned to stay there until my money ran out. But as my money ran out, I realized I wasn't ready to return home. So, I needed to find a way to make money. And so that began as a job I found online writing for sex toy websites! I was the 'Ask Alice' of the online sex toy industry, and it was fun! But it wasn't steady enough work. So, I got a second job teaching English to kids at GEE English School on the weekends. But I didn't like working the weekends that much, especially with kids who didn't want to be there, and so I kept looking for new opportunities.

Eventually, I was offered a job at a German company in Chiang Mai that let me keep my writing job (I could actually do it *while* at the other job, so I was getting paid twice) and that was awesome! And it was often boring, and it didn't challenge me in any way. Then I got a job as a PR assistant at a global drug and alcohol rehab facility as the content creation and digital marketing manager. It was a great job with good pay, and I was learning a lot. But by this point I hadn't been home in a couple years, and I only received three weeks' vacation with that job, which just wasn't enough when you're flying literally around the world to get home. So, I bargained with my manager to work remotely. He wasn't keen at first, so I made him a deal – I'd take half my salary for the first three months to prove to him that I would do an equal or better job and we could reassess after. He was surprised to see that my work actually improved when I left the office, and so there I was with a job that allowed me to travel the world and work at the same time.

Ahh … Finally!

Learning to Ebb and Flow with Life

That is just a small example of how I've learned to ebb and flow in my life. And I tell you this because people have often said to me, 'You're so lucky', or 'Things just fall into your lap.' But my life isn't what it is today based on luck, or things just falling into my lap. Things are the way they are in my life because I am open to change instead of resisting it. I ebb and flow with the ebb and flow of life. I pay attention to signs and messages from the universe and do what feels right in the moment rather than overthinking and getting stuck in what I *should* do or worrying about what *might* happen.

What if I'd held tight to the idea that I was *supposed to* stay in Australia for a year? What if I fought against my heart with my logical mind, saying, 'Kandis, you paid for this visa to work here, and the flight to get here, it's foolish to go back to Chiang Mai. You can't even work there!" Or what if, when I was running out of money in Chiang Mai, I decided to go home instead of finding a way to make money and stay?

I guarantee you wouldn't be sitting here reading this book.

That time in my life changed me, and I had to let go of so much of what I thought things would look like in order to take the steps I did to get me where I am today. And gee, golly, gosh I'm sure glad I did. That experience created a version of me that I am simply in love with. And I had to let go of A LOT to get here. I let go of beliefs, ideas, even ways of being that were no longer serving me.

Letting go and accepting change is one of the hardest things that people struggle with. We quickly develop deep attachment to people, places, ideas, and beliefs. Deep attachments to who we think we are. And when we are met with the need to let them go, we hold on tight. But why?

When we learn to let go of what is no longer serving us, we're making room in our life for what will take us to the next level. And the more we learn to let go quickly and with ease, the brighter our future will be.

The Theories Behind Chapter 7

Letting go of someone I was still in love with wasn't easy.

It wasn't easy letting go of my fiancé a few years before that either.

It wasn't easy telling my family and friends that I was leaving for a year-long trip around the world. And it especially wasn't easy telling them I'd decided to stay even longer.

It wasn't easy when I made the decision to leave Thailand and come home to North America to focus on my career and everything that entailed.

It wasn't easy when I had to tell everyone that I'd decided to go to Italy instead.

And it definitely wasn't easy when I arrived back in Canada after seven years of living abroad to stay in a bedroom in my mom and dad's basement with my parents, my twenty-year-old niece, and her newborn baby all living under the same roof.

It wasn't easy letting go of my beliefs that home should have changed either.

Saying goodbye to friends each time I left for a new country wasn't exactly easy either. Nor was it easy to come home seven years after I'd first left, feeling like a completely changed person from everything I'd experienced just to realize that home was exactly the same as it was when I left it. And it wasn't easy letting go of my beliefs that home *should have* changed either.

Getting to know myself in such a deep way over the past decade and letting go of parts of who I was along the way was not easy.

In fact, at times it was quite uncomfortable and sometimes even painful. But it also allowed me to accept change and let things go so much more easily than I once would have been able to do.

Most of the time when we find ourselves resisting change or experiencing difficulty in letting go, it's because we can't imagine, or we fear how our life would be if that change were to happen.

The Difficulties of Letting Go

Letting go can be one of the hardest things for us humans to do. But when we get the hang of it, it becomes incredibly freeing.

We tend to fear letting go because we are scared of the change that it will create – we are scared of what might come next. For many, it's easier to keep hanging on to what's familiar than to let go and see what happens when we try something new.

And learning to let go easily is one of the most beneficial things we can do.

There's an old wisdom tale that I first heard from James Wedmore that goes something like this...

> Each day this boy walked through town past Old Joe's place. Old Joe would sit on his front porch with a dog sitting next to him. And each day the boy walked past, Old Joe would be rocking back and forth in his rocking chair and the dog would be howling and whimpering. One day the boy finally asked, 'What's wrong with your dog?' and Old Joe replied simply, 'He's sitting on a nail.' 'Well why doesn't he move?' the boy asked. 'Because it doesn't hurt bad enough,' said Old Joe.

Holding On to Pain

It seems silly to think that people will hold on to pain simply because it's 'not bad enough', right? But it's more common than we think. In fact, most people are allowing some type of pain to be present most of the time.

For example, back when I was still living in Toronto, I was working a job and living a life I didn't like. I was drowning my mental pain in drugs, alcohol, and shopping. And yet until that fateful day at the bar with a stranger, I didn't realize there was any other option. And thus, for a long time I held on to the pain that I knew.

Let me ask you:

Have you ever thought you might have a cavity because you notice some sensitivity, but you put off going to the dentist to find out for sure? When the cavity became inflamed and painful with everything you tried to eat or drink, chances are you booked an appointment immediately, right? The subtle pain you knew was no longer bearable. It became too much and you finally took action.

Or what about this:

Have you ever stayed in a romantic relationship that was making you miserable because the thought of not having them around and living life on your own seemed worse? Or perhaps you wanted a divorce, but the looming legal battle encouraged you to continue with the relationship instead?

Or how long have you stayed at a job that made you cringe as you walked in the door? You hated the job, or perhaps you're still there and you still hate the job. But every time you think about quitting and getting a new one, you fear the possibility that you won't get a new one. That you're not good enough for anything else, or nothing else is available. Perhaps just the idea of creating a resume and going for job interviews seems like too much. And so you stay in the pain of a job you hate because you can't envision the possibility of greater things to come your way.

For many, the pain we know is better than the pain we don't know

At least, that's what our brain tells us.

Our brain has been hardwired to constantly seek out danger. Why? So that it can respond quickly *if* it notices any. Which of course, in turn, helps to keep us alive and out of harm's way.

However, there's a bit of glitch.

Our brain perceives anything unknown as 'more dangerous than where/how we are now', simply because we're clearly alive in that moment and if we change things up, danger could be ahead. So at the most basic and primitive level, this is why uncertainty and change can feel so scary. Our brain is sending signals saying, 'But we're safe here. Why would you move? What if we're not safe *there?*'

Dr. Rick Hanson says in his book, *The Buddha's Brain:*

"The brain is Velcro for negative experiences and Teflon for positive ones."

Because of this natural instinct to constantly look out for danger (aka keep us alive), we are more prone to notice and remember negative experiences in our life. So, our brain is more apt to remember that one time in Grade 2 that we told someone that we loved them and they didn't love us back – rather than the 50 times in the next 20 years we told someone we loved them and they *did* love us back.

Just like the brain doesn't want physical danger, it doesn't want emotional danger either. So rather than chance a higher dose of pain by letting go of certain things and creating change, our brain's automatic choice is to stay in the pain we know.

Which keeps us 'stuck', unable to let go, and invite change in.

But just like everything else we've discussed in this book – you are not your brain. You are not your thoughts. And so you must challenge these ideas too.

How Long Will You Sit in that Familiar Pain?

Just like the dog sitting on the nail, I'm curious …

How long are you willing to sit in pain because you're too damn scared to see what's on the other side of that door?

How long are you going to tell yourself that sitting in pain is okay? That it's better than doing something new?

How long will you tell yourself that you're not '*really*' in pain?

How long will you tell yourself that there's not much you can do about it? That this is just how life is?

We can become so attached to this pain, that the thought of not experiencing it can actually leave us in fear that we won't recognize who we are without it. The pain has become part of our identity. It is through the pain that the ego has created its (and your) place in this world.

Your Pain Can Become Your Identity

I used to work at what I called a flower factory. It was a greenhouse technically, but I just worked on the factory line that packaged the plants in pretty cellophane wrappers before being boxed up and shipped out to stores. And there was this guy there. He started talking to me my first or second day about what a terrible place the factory was, and how he was quitting in the next couple of weeks because he just couldn't stand the place anymore. And then when he walked away, one of the ladies beside me who'd worked there for years rolled her eyes and said, "Don't mind him. He's been saying that exact same thing for the past two years." His hate for the job has simply become a part of who he is.

Or maybe you can think of a friend you have now or in the past who, every time you speak, they go on and on about their spouse or their partner, complaining about everything they do, the arguments they have, and how they'd be better off single. And yet for the past five years you've been having this exact same conversation with them. This love/hate relationship has become a part of their identity. They don't know how to actually leave it anymore.

We become so attached to who we are when we're experiencing that pain, that we often can't see it. We've become so attached to this pain it's as though we've completely *become* it.

Attachment

There's an exercise I learned from one of my teachers that I love doing with groups of students in a live workshop. When the students enter the room, there are images ripped out from magazines and books, and they're spread out all over the tables or on the floor. I invite my students to spend a few minutes finding two pictures: a picture they really like, and a picture they really don't like. Preferably an image that evokes an emotional response, either highly positive or highly negative. There's no need to understand why it does what it does, just as long as it does it.

Then I'll suggest they go back to their seats and put the image they don't like face up on the desk in front of them, and the other image out of sight. I'll ask them to simply gaze at this image in silence for a few moments. And then I'll request they pick up the image and rip it apart, creating as many or as few pieces as they like.

Once they've all finished, I'll ask them to then put the image that evoked a positive response in front of them. Once again we sit in silence as they soak up the image and everything it makes them feel. And once again I'll ask them to pick up the image and rip it apart, creating as many or as few pieces as they like.

And every time, the results are the same.

When I ask them to rip up the image that brings up a negative emotion, they are quite quick to do so. In fact, most are quite happy to do it. Some rip it up into tiny pieces so that you can't tell what the image ever was, and some rip it with a clear aggression and urgency. They sit back when they're done, a look of satisfaction and calm across their face and in their body language.

Then when I ask them to rip up the image that brings up a positive emotion, I am almost always met with a room full of questioning eyes looking up at me. They stare at me, eyes wide, as they hesitate to rip the image. I'll usually have one person speak up.

"Do we have to?" they'll ask.

"You don't have to," I'll reply, "but I'm asking you to."

And so they begin to rip the image. Most often it's ripped much slower than the other image, and in larger pieces as if they might put it back together again later. They'll place it to the side when they're done, sitting back in their chairs this time, but not with a sense of satisfaction, it's a far more unsettling energy in the room.

And when we open the floor to discussion it becomes apparent that they quickly developed an attachment to a ripped up magazine picture they'd only just laid eyes on a few moments before. An almost instant attachment that caused them to resist my request to rip it up. And they didn't even know that this image existed a mere 10 minutes prior. They had no plans for it in the future, but this moment of positive emotional connection caused them to feel sad about ripping it up. And not only sad, but some students will even tell me that when I told them to rip it up, they felt a flicker of anger or annoyance toward me for asking them to do it. Wild, isn't it? How quickly we can become so attached to something.

But it's important to note that it wasn't just the lack of wanting to rip the positive image that shows attachment, because look how quickly they also turned the other image into an enemy. With that image they were excited to rip it up, shred it, get rid of it. "Good riddance," one might say. This strong need to get rid of an image they just found on the ground moments before, is most definitely another example of attachment.

And to see how quickly this emotional trigger to a random image can cause a human to behave so differently to one than the other – imagine how often this is happening in our regular life. We form judgments and beliefs so quickly and then have difficulty letting that shit go.

"Attachment is the root of all suffering." —Buddha

I mentioned this concept previously and it's worth mentioning again. Pain is unavoidable when living a human life. But suffering is optional.

Suffering = Pain x Resistance

And at the root cause of pain is attachment. Attachment to other people, attachment to places, attachment to things, and attachment to who we believe ourselves to be (or want to be) – attachment to our own identity. When things we are attached to begin to change, it's not uncommon to experience an emotional response – often sadness or anger. Just like when I asked the group to rip the images, there was an emotional response involved that was created in just a few moments.

And there's nothing wrong with emotional responses to people, places or things. In fact, life would be pretty boring without them. But there is a big difference between a healthy emotional response and an emotional attachment.

An emotional response means that when you see or are near a person, place, or thing, emotion rises within you.

An emotional connection is when you feel lightly or deeply connected to another person, place or thing on an emotional level.

An emotional attachment is when you fear that your life won't be as good if that person, place or thing does not exist within it. That without this person, place, or thing, you will be 'missing something'. It can often resemble clinging, or a *need to keep* some thing or some one around.

It's often that moment when you realize something is changing and your mind suddenly is filled with what could have, should have, or would have been.

Some people will argue that certain levels of emotional attachment are healthy. I disagree.

Emotional response and emotional connection? Heck yes.

Attachment? No.

Things are *always* changing. And when we become attached to anything, we are putting our security, happiness, and comfort in the hands of someone or something else. And when we do that, we are giving away our power and resisting the ebb and flow of this life in our universe.[4]

And attachment can come in many forms.

Attachment to Things

Things, things, things. We are living in a material world ... and it's common for people to get very attached to things.

Have you ever seen the show *Hoarders*? The people in that show can barely move around the house because of all the things they have collected over the years, and when the host of the show comes on and starts helping them sort through to get rid of some of the things, they come under serious mental distress at the thought of getting rid of anything. Each newspaper or mug or old sweater has a story, and they feel like they literally can't get rid of it or their world will come crashing down.

For most people, it doesn't get to the level of the people on *Hoarders*. But that doesn't mean that probably every single one of you reading this book has at least one thing tucked away somewhere in your house that you're only keeping because it has 'sentimental value'.

And don't get me wrong, there's nothing wrong with that. But what if it breaks? How will you react? Your reaction is the indicator of your attachment. For example, let's say you have a mug that you just bought at the Dollar Store a couple days ago. You're doing the dishes and you accidentally drop it on the floor, and it smashes. Maybe you're annoyed that you've got to sweep the floor, but you have no emotional response to the mug itself. Now imagine that

---

4   Please note: I'm speaking completely separate from the psychology of attachment theory with which I fully agree. In this case, I'm speaking to grown adults developing attachment to people, places, or things.

you're doing the dishes and drop the mug that your late grandmother gave to you for your birthday the year before she passed – and it smashes all over the floor.

How emotional do you get?

I've seen some people break down in complete puddles of sobs and cry for an hour. This, as you may have guessed, is high level attachment to an inanimate object. We *attach* a memory or a feeling to the object and if something happens to it or for some reason we have to get rid of it, it becomes upsetting.

Attachment to People

People are easy to get attached to, right? We're in a relationship, and the thought of not having that person around can be heartbreaking. Or a family member passes away, and we completely break down. Some people will mourn these losses for years. Some even decades. But just like the mug, we are mourning our stories more than the actual person.

Now hear me out.

My great-grandmother always used to tell me, "If you can't laugh, you might as well be dead." I loved that saying, and I even have it tattooed on my ribcage. She was always a jolly, positive woman, and one day when I was about seventeen, and she was getting older, I was tucking her into bed. And she took my hand and looked me in the eye, and she said, "Kandis, I can't laugh anymore."

It broke my heart. This jolly, positive, happy woman was telling me she was ready for death to take her away. And a week or so later she died peacefully in her sleep.

Now, she was one of my favorite humans I've had the opportunity to get to know in this lifetime, and I remember as we prepared for her funeral, I asked my mom if something was wrong with me because I didn't feel sad – but rather I felt peace. I felt at peace knowing that this woman who lived her life to laugh could no longer laugh and she was rewarded her request to live no more.

My mom assured me there was nothing wrong with me, saying that it was actually 'quite mature' and she was proud of me.

Of course, I've missed Nanna at certain events, or wished for her presence here and there, but ultimately it was her time to go. She was ready, and so I chose to be ready too. But what often happens is that we resist what is. When we lose someone we love – either from death or a broken relationship – we get consumed in the thoughts of what could have been, should have been, or would have been if things were different. We start to imagine all the ways in which our life will change, or we'll miss them in the future – and we stay emotionally attached to them. But when they're gone, this attachment only continues to provide us with suffering.

And so of course we must take the time to grieve. But we also must accept the moment for what it is and notice any thoughts that come up for us that are wishing for things to be the way they aren't so that we can allow ourselves to adapt and move forward.

Attachment to Meaning

We *loooove* to attach meaning to things. Especially words.

Watch this.

Read each color in the list below individually and notice the first thing that comes to mind. For example, you read the color 'orange' and you might immediately think 'tiger', or 'orange juice', or 'basketball'. Don't overthink it. Just notice the first word or image that comes up.

Write it down if you like.

red
purple
black
blue
green
maroon
aqua

So what did you come up with? I love doing this exercise with a group of people because we always get such a variety of words associated with each color. Since we're not in a group to illustrate this, I just did the exercise as I wrote this instead, and these were the associations that came up for me: red – blood, purple – dragon, black – death, blue – butterfly, green – grass, maroon – sexy, aqua – rings.

Did any of mine match yours?

There's a small chance you might have gotten one or two the same, but most often the majority of answers are completely different. Because we each put our own meaning on words based on our past experience, our physical and emotional state, and our learned ideas, morals, and beliefs.

And we can even take this further. When I thought of 'death' for the color black, some people might think that was morbid. But when I think of death I see the lighter side. I see that on the opposite side of death is life. And death is a reminder to me to always live my best life. It's a large part of why I love skull rings and have integrated skulls into my home decor. Death isn't sad or morbid to me, but rather a reminder to live my life to the fullest, to say what I want to say, and to go for my dreams.

So we must be careful what we attach to words – especially when they're coming out of someone else's mouth, because we have *no idea* what that meaning is for them. You can make it mean whatever you want. It's a great tool to use when someone says something that hurts you. Flip the meaning!

> *Be careful what we attach to words – especially when they're coming out of someone else's mouth, because we have no idea what that meaning is for them.*

Attachment to Ideas and Beliefs

This is a huge one.

Ideas and beliefs.

Or in other words – stories.

Stories that we've created in our creative little mind about how the world works.

And while they're just thoughts and creations of our own, these can be some of the hardest things to let go. In fact, wars have been started over attachment to beliefs and ideas. Remember, our ego has been collecting beliefs about us and the world since we first arrived on this planet. But not all of them are helpful. In fact, a lot of them aren't.

For example, if you grew up in a home where your parents didn't have a lot of money, and they said things like, 'Money doesn't grow on trees', or 'Money doesn't come easy.' then what beliefs do you think you'll likely adapt as you grow up? And if you're thinking that it's difficult to receive money, what type of energetic vibration do you think you're putting out into the world? One of 'money is hard to get', right? And the universe delivers what you put out.

"But money IS hard to come by!" I can hear some of you thinking right now.

And to that I say, 'But what if it wasn't?' What might change for you if you began to believe that money could come easily?

Just because you've seen something to be true in the past, doesn't mean it will always be in the future. Learn to notice your limiting beliefs and then drop your attachment to them. Let them go and see what becomes possible for you when you do.

Attachment to Expectations

There's a saying I've heard in life that the only way to avoid disappointment is to not have any expectations.

I used to think that sounded very melancholy and even a bit depressing. 'What is life without expectations?' I always thought.

But now I see the power in dropping expectations. Because the problem with expectations is that most of them are unsaid.

I know people who have spent their entire lives full of anger, sadness, and resentment because their parents didn't live up to their expectations. "A good

We can request something from someone, and if they say yes, then we've created an agreement. But until then, it's an unsaid expectation.

parent would have done this ... or a good parent would have done that."

Or the way I got upset with Pablo when I started creating a new vision for the future and didn't tell him about it but expected him to just start going forward with it.

We can request something from someone, and if they say yes, then we've created an agreement. But until then, it's an unsaid expectation. And we have to let go of attachment to expectations. Even the ones on ourselves and our own life. One of the reasons we have

Let go of how you think it should be, and experience it for what it is.

such difficulty breaking up with someone or leaving a job you thought was going to be your dream job but it turns out that it sucks is because we're attached to what we *expected* it to be.

Instead, expect the unexpected. Learn that nothing in the universe is ever exactly what you expect it to be, and learn to stop expecting things from yourself, situations, and others.

Life is What We Make It

When we hold on to things that are no longer serving us, we never live to our utmost potential or achieve the joy, happiness, and success in our life that we desire.

If something is no longer serving you in your life, let it go!

Don't allow it to take up your energy or change your vibrational frequency.

We fear change, but change is actually amazing because it means there is always a new opportunity waiting around the corner for you. We create our own reality, and the fact that everything is always changing means that we have an opportunity in each moment to create a more desirable reality.

Everything is always changing – change is inevitable

According to the teachings of the Buddha, life is comparable to a river. It is a progressive moment, a successive series of different moments, joining together to give the impression of one continuous flow. It moves from cause to cause, effect to effect, one point to another, one state of existence to another, giving an outward impression that it is one continuous and unified movement, whereas in reality it is not. The river of yesterday is not the same as the river of today. The river of this moment is not going to be the same as the river of the next moment. So does life. It changes continuously, becomes something or the other from moment to moment.[5]

And so it is with humans too.

To think that the person we are now is the same person we were yesterday is absurd. The person you are in this moment is not the same person you were just a moment before, or a moment before that, and you're not now the same person you will be in a few moments' time.

In other words, we are constantly changing.

If this book is living with the intention I had for it, then your ideas and beliefs about life are being challenged. It's guiding you to think in new ways. You will never be the same person you were before picking it up. And even if you hated every word you've read so far,

---

5   Jayaram V, "Anicca or Anitya in Buddhism," accessed February 3, 2021, https://www.hinduwebsite.com/buddhism/anicca.asp

you're still a new person because you're now a person who had their thoughts and ideas challenged by a book that you hated.

But beyond the way in which we think, we're physically changing too. As you read these words on this page, cells in your body are dividing. Some cells are dying. Some are arising anew. Your body is aging as we speak. So are the pages on which this book is written, or the electronic device on which you read it or listen to these words. The food in your fridge is becoming less fresh. The seasons are slowly changing, the planet is spinning, and nothing – literally nothing – will ever be exactly as it was even just one second ago.

> *Those who suffer the most, suffer because they resist this change that, in essence, is life.*

Every being and every thing is different *in this moment* than it was a moment ago.

And now again in this moment, everything is different once again.

This moment too.

And this one.

And on it goes … because *nothing* will ever be exactly the same way as it ever once was.

For some, this idea induces fear.

But for what reason?

These are simply the facts of life – it's just the way things are!

Those who suffer the most, suffer because they resist this change that, in essence, *is life.*

And yet the interesting paradox is that the more we resist change, or wish for things to stay the same, the more we actually notice the change and become affected by it. Because what we resist persists. Our energy goes where our attention flows. And so when we become all consumed with fear of change, we see it even more than ever before.

Think back for a moment to the happiest time of your life.

Now think about the fact that you'll never experience that moment ever again.

Notice how that feels for you.

Now, think back for a moment to the worst time of your life.

And know now that you'll never experience that moment ever again either.

Notice how that feels for you.

People often see change as something to be sad about, or even to fear. But what if change was the most beautiful thing in the world?

If change is inevitable, and change is always happening, how can we harness that power to create change in our future that exhilarates us, and lights us up with joy in each moment?

How can we learn to flow *with* the change instead of resisting it?

When we embrace the fact that everything is changing in every moment, and that things will never be the same, we can let things go with greater ease because we never had the expectation of them to stick around in the first place.

When we feel anxiety about change in our life, we must acknowledge that the change already happened, or is currently happening. Then we must simply accept it. You must move forward exactly as though you had chosen it.

Because what's the alternative?

$$Suffering = Pain \times Resistance$$

When we choose to accept the present moment as if we'd chosen it, we release the resistance, which releases the suffering.

It means that we get to choose a new meaning for ourselves.

For example, let's say you're getting a divorce. You could make it mean that you've failed, that you'll be alone forever, and that you're not worthy of love. Or, more realistically (and positive too) you could make it mean simply that you're no longer married, you've got to hire a lawyer, and potentially find a new place to live. You could also choose to see it as a new chapter full of new possibilities and fulfillment of new dreams.

It is literally *your choice*.

And one of the best ways to find acceptance is to focus on the details in the present moment.

Break it down into the steps that you need to take to get through the immediate situation and look for things that you could deem as positive. *Get specific.*

> **The only things we have control over in this life are our own actions, thoughts, and behaviors.**

When you're finding your new place after the divorce, revel in the fact that you get to choose the exact furnishings and decor you want – no compromise! You get to choose the movie you want to watch, and it doesn't mean that next time you have to watch one that you *don't* want to watch.

When you are able to see the positive aspects in what seems like an otherwise dire situation, you can start to truly feel like you *did* choose this after all. Because remember – the *only* things we have control over in this life are our own actions, thoughts, and behaviors.

So when we can accept change as if we'd chosen it – whether we did initially or not – we can release the attachment to how we thought things would go, or how things 'should be', and we can feel more positive and at peace in the present moment.

Acknowledge, Accept, Release

There's a three-step process I've been using when it comes to 'negative' situations in life that cannot be changed. If you recall from earlier in the book, I mentioned that when we're met with what we perceive as a negative life situation, the first thing we must do is ask ourselves if we can do anything to change it. If the answer is no, then we apply this three-step process:

Step 1: Acknowledge that there is something in your life situation that you're not pleased about. It's there, it's real, it's happening, and it can't be changed by your actions or words.

Step 2: Accept it as if you'd chosen it. Perhaps you even want to say out loud, "I choose _____", or my favorite, "So this is what's happening is it? *Okay, let's go!*"

Step 3: Release your attachment to it being any other way. Let go of your expectations or ideas of how it could have, should have, or would have gone.

And that's it! Simple!

Simple, but not always easy.

Key Takeaway

Good news! The more you practice this process, the easier it becomes. And of course, it all becomes easier when we learn to quiet our mind – quiet those racing thoughts – so we don't get whisked away by unhelpful stories of what could have been.

> *"You can't call it 'the past' until you leave it behind. Until then, it's called the present."*
>
> —Nina, *Offspring*

CHAPTER 8

Ten Days of Silence

My leg muscles are really sore, and now that he [my teacher] has increased my practice to 20 minutes each of standing and sitting meditation, my legs/feet fall completely asleep by the end of my sitting meditation …

… I can't believe I have five more full days here! How did I end up getting so into this last time? Am I going to have a breakthrough this time? I'm starting to think I won't and five more nights of sleeping here is not sounding like very much fun! Maybe I'm putting too much pressure on myself because last time I had a change on the fourth day which is tomorrow. I feel like I'm failing! I wish I'd read my notes from last year, but then maybe it's best to just do what feels right in the moment …

… I'm so hungry. I thought I'd be used to this by now.

I can't wait to get that Vietnamese herb salad from Blue Diamond as soon as I get out of here …

… I'm scared that I'm thinking I will achieve something here that I won't. I just have to tell myself that I hated the first three days last time too. I'm not that bad this time anyways. It's 7p.m. and I'm in bed. I'm hoping my calves & my hip joint won't hurt so much tomorrow. My right leg is seriously painful right now.

It seemed that I'd finally found what that temple on the top of the mountain had in store for me. It was a 10-day silent vipassana meditation retreat – twice.

There I was, lying on a small single bed, in a room with nothing else in it, atop Chiang Mai's tallest mountain in one of Thailand's most famous temples, and I was wondering what in the hell ever possessed me to come back to this retreat.

10 days in silence.

10 days of 8 hours a day (or more) of meditation.

10 days of waking up at 5 a.m. and not eating anything past noon.

My legs were so sore that I was rubbing Tiger Balm on them constantly, massaging them and stretching them every chance I got.

I'd been there the previous year, and so while I technically knew what to expect of my stay, there was a level of disbelief in that moment that I had returned. To anyone who has ever done a 10-day Vipassana retreat and says, "It was so amazing. Such a relaxing experience!" I find it difficult to believe you were actually doing the work.

Just a few days earlier I was shopping for meditation clothes in the busy city markets with my friend and Chiang Mai local, Earth. The meditation center requires plain white clothing for the duration of your stay, and while my Thai vocabulary was improving, it was helpful to have Earth guide me toward the traditional clothing specifically made for this purpose. I purchased two sets for a total of twelve dollars. The following day, he took me into town where I could catch a songthaew up the mountain to the temple that had left me completely breathless so many years before.

And gosh, was I nervous! It felt like the first time all over again. I was simultaneously excited and scared as heck for the upcoming days. It's not an easy process, and I kept thinking, "What did I get myself into?"

Finally, the songthaew stopped at the bottom of that grand staircase with the dragons carved into the railings and 309 steps to the majestic temple I loved so dearly. With my tiny backpack of simple toiletries, some laundry soap, a thermal tea mug, my journal, and the white clothes I'd purchased, I began to climb those stairs for one of the most life-changing and challenging experiences of my life.

It was mid-April, which means the hot season was well underway, and I was soaked in sweat by the time I reached the top of those stairs. When I got to the ticket booth where I normally had to pay a fee for entry, I was waved past the booth and given directions to the meditation hall and sleeping quarters away from the main temple and tourist attractions. As I stepped off the main route and began following the signs for the meditation hall, the bustling sounds from the temple became quieter and quieter as I walked down a path frequently obstructed by plants, random pipes, or broken concrete. "This surely would get someone sued or closed down back home," I thought for probably the millionth time since I'd arrived in Thailand.

The path continued to weave down, until I finally saw a series of buildings built up the side of the mountain and surrounded by exotic trees and greenery, vines hanging down from the tree branches. The trees swayed and danced in the light breeze, and I could see a monkey swinging far below, and birds singing and dancing everywhere as I pushed open the door to the main office of the meditation center.

There were signs on the door, the walls, and on the front desk reminding us not to speak unless necessary. I filled out some forms in silence and was handed our daily schedule and a room key. I was instructed to get settled in my room and change into my white clothing before meeting back in the main hall that afternoon for our introductions and ceremony.

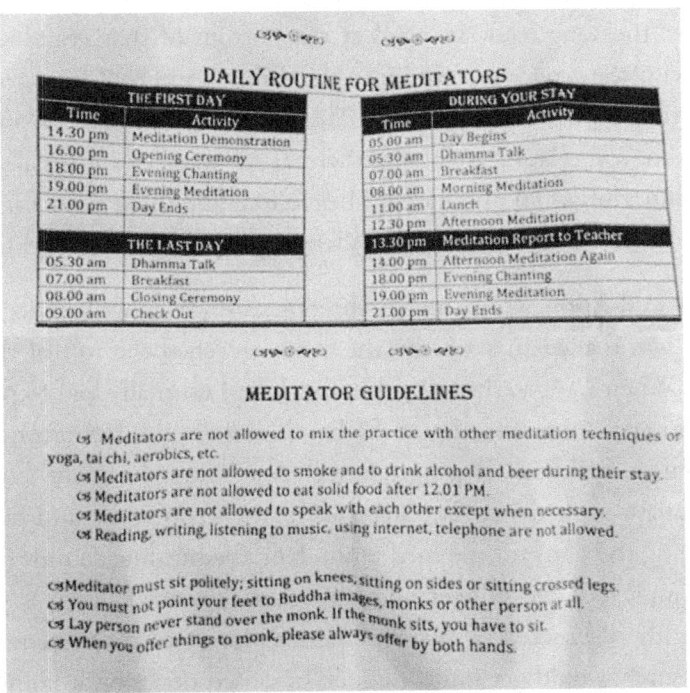

DAILY ROUTINE FOR MEDITATORS

THE FIRST DAY		DURING YOUR STAY	
Time	Activity	Time	Activity
14.30 pm	Meditation Demonstration	05.00 am	Day Begins
16.00 pm	Opening Ceremony	05.30 am	Dhamma Talk
18.00 pm	Evening Chanting	07.00 am	Breakfast
19.00 pm	Evening Meditation	08.00 am	Morning Meditation
21.00 pm	Day Ends	11.00 am	Lunch
		12.30 pm	Afternoon Meditation
THE LAST DAY		13.30 pm	Meditation Report to Teacher
05.30 am	Dhamma Talk	14.00 pm	Afternoon Meditation Again
07.00 am	Breakfast	18.00 pm	Evening Chanting
08.00 am	Closing Ceremony	19.00 pm	Evening Meditation
09.00 am	Check Out	21.00 pm	Day Ends

MEDITATOR GUIDELINES

ᘿ Meditators are not allowed to mix the practice with other meditation techniques or yoga, tai chi, aerobics, etc.
ᘿ Meditators are not allowed to smoke and to drink alcohol and beer during their stay.
ᘿ Meditators are not allowed to eat solid food after 12.01 PM.
ᘿ Meditators are not allowed to speak with each other except when necessary.
ᘿ Reading, writing, listening to music, using internet, telephone are not allowed.

ᘿ Meditator must sit politely; sitting on knees, sitting on sides or sitting crossed legs.
ᘿ You must not point your feet to Buddha images, monks or other person at all.
ᘿ Lay person never stand over the monk. If the monk sits, you have to sit.
ᘿ When you offer things to monk, please always offer by both hands.

Our daily schedule (I adhered to all the rules except for 'writing'. I kept a journal each day, so I could remember what I had experienced, and what the teacher taught us. I did my best to keep the writing factual and minimal, without allowing my mind to wander too much in thought or creativity.)

As I removed my shoes and stepped into my private bedroom, I was pleasantly surprised by what I saw. It was very clean and simple. A small basic single bed in the corner with sheets and a pillow. And that was it. I dropped my bag, and as I walked to the bathrooms at the end of the open-air hallway, I recalled my apprehension the year before, wondering if I would find squatters or Western toilets. And as I turned the corner, I was once again pleasantly surprised to find the bathrooms clean with Western toilets instead of squatters. YAY!

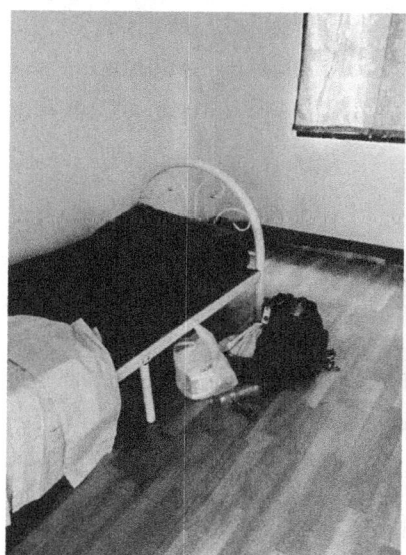

Image caption (left): My minimalistic bedroom for the 10-day retreat.
Image caption (right): Outside my room was one of my favorite places to practice.

I went back to my room to get dressed, and suddenly felt all the nerves rise up within me. I was nervous about what I would go through mentally in the next ten days, but I also felt a sense of warmth and familiarity to be back in this magical place.

Filled with Purpose, Love, and Light

The opening ceremony came and went, and as I walked up to the main meditation hall at 6 p.m. for chanting, I remembered how lost and confused I had been at this point the year before. Each night, we sat in rows on pillows on the floor chanting from a book in which the 'lyrics' were written in phonetic tones of a language I didn't know. At first I felt awkward and uncomfortable, but I soon found that the practice of chanting in itself was an exercise in letting go of the need to follow the lyrics and know what I was doing, and instead immerse myself in the sounds and vibrations of the others chanting – and when I let go of the desire to control, I was able to ebb and flow with the rest of them, and it began to feel very natural, easy, and beautiful.

That first night of my second retreat I walked hurriedly to the hall excited to immerse myself back in the chanting. It took me a few minutes to get the hang of it once again, but it felt amazing when I did. Once the chanting was complete, we would sit and listen to our teacher's Dhamma talk, which covered Buddhist principles and ideas, wisdom tales, and practices to live a healthy life with peace of mind.

It felt so good to be back, and I left the meditation hall that night with a glow radiating from inside of me as if I were filled with purpose, love, and light.

And It was Also Very Challenging

Each day was the same. Sometimes I did my daily meditations inside the meditation hall, and other days I would set up some pillows outside my room on the balcony and meditate below the sounds of the jungle high up on the mountain.

During those ten days of silence, as I asked my mind to quiet its racing thoughts, I had fleeting moments of what seemed like a peacefulness and calm that took over my mind and body and connected me across spiritual realms in our universe. I experienced feelings that I was not just connected to everything in the universe, but I was literally a *part of it*. And if I was lucky, these moments might last ten or fifteen minutes out of 8–10 hours of meditation each day.

The rest of the time, as I encouraged my mind to become quiet, it chose instead to recall memories of events that I often didn't even know I'd experienced. I received small flashbacks or full movies of my childhood playing out like a film before my (closed) eyes. Or I'd be struck with the most creative and wonderful business ideas mid-session. The quieter I asked my mind to become, and the longer the periods of silence I could create, the more intense the visions and ideas became in between.

On a particularly non-quiet-mind kind of day, I drew this in my journal ...

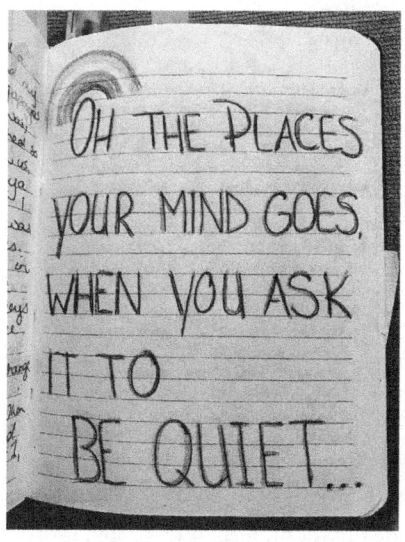

And this...

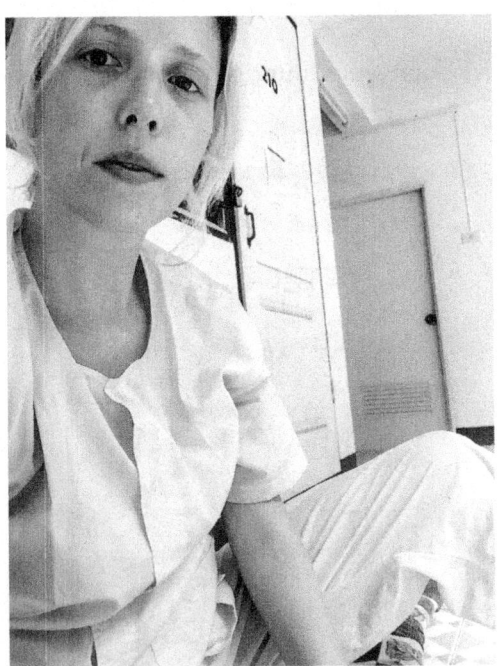

> PoS. This is an emotional,
> exhausting journey.

It's not often we give ourselves the space to sit for three hours or more at a time with nowhere to go, nowhere to be, no phone, no book, no art supplies ... just an invitation to dive deep within.

An invitation to be still, and simply ask your mind to stop thinking so much.

To offer the mind an opportunity to become clear, and simply focus on noticing your breath.

Me, outside my room, feeling frustrated on Day 2 or 3.

And it's not always easy. It really shows us what a fast-paced world we live in when suddenly we're literally doing *nothing* all day. The benefits of these retreats are indescribable, and invaluable, and they are not easy. I could tell when the new retreat members were on their third day, because when we were inside the meditation hall for our dhamma talks or chanting, they couldn't sit still. They were rubbing their legs, massaging them, trying to take away the pain. For all those hours of meditation we were seated cross-legged or we were balancing on one leg for our walking meditations. For eight hours a day or more. The legs get sore, the mind gets frustrated, and you can often uncover memories that you buried deep down inside sometime long ago.

And through all the uncertainty, the frustration, and the physical pain that you could see in the journal entry to start this chapter, I also received a deep sense of peace. It was incredibly hard

> *It becomes a practice of acceptance, patience, and letting go*

to slow down to such a pace, but it eventually became enjoyable. I found myself fascinated by the natural world around me and noticed things I wouldn't normally have given the time of day to. I spent almost an hour one day on my hands and knees outside my room watching ants. Have you ever wondered how you can drop a crumb of food and within minutes there is a whole swarm of ants carrying it away? I watched long enough and close enough to see them communicate with their antennas, develop a plan, and call just enough ants to carry each piece back to the colony.

I found myself lost without thought, simply watching the leaves blow, the birds fly, and the natural world unfold around me. The difficulty and struggle I found in the beginning dissipated by about the fifth or sixth day, and was replaced by a sense of wonder, perhaps even magic, toward the world around me.

My journal entry from the last day of my first retreat on April 11, 2016:

> I am in a very positive space and looking forward to chanting tonight … Last night we went to join a ceremony at the main temple, and I can't explain my emotions that overcame me. As the monks began to chat, the wind picked up and small bells began to ring. And as the chanting quieted down, the wind and the chime of the bells did too. It was as though just the energy of those chants had brought the temple to life.
>
> It is a night that I will remember forever. And even if just for that one experience, this whole thing would have been worth it, but I'm taking away so much more than that …
>
> … Everything always just seems to work out great in life, you know? Even when the bad things come, you have got to just take them in stride and focus on the positive. Thank you, world, for being with me, and thank you Buddha for helping me find the way.
>
> *LIFE IS A MIRACLE!*
>
> *BE GRATEFUL EVERY DAY!*
>
> *I am so blessed.*
>
> I feel like the heavens are shining down on me these past few days.
>
> I am just so lucky to be alive.
>
> I'm lying here crying tears of joy.

What an experience this has been!"

My journal entry from the last day of my second retreat on April 17, 2017:

What a great story to end my stay with! It rained all night, and we woke up to no electricity. We had our Dhamma talk by the light of one giant yellow candle. I don't think it could have been more perfect. At one point he (the teacher) looked right at me and said, 'In Buddhism we have something called 'release'. It means, let it be …'

I just felt that today especially, but this whole week too, that I feel like such a good fit. I am exactly where I'm supposed to be. I have been practicing many of these things for over a decade, but now feel like I can explain the concepts better, and he has awakened me more deeply to them. This was a roller coaster of a week, but once again I am so happy that I did this!

I'M SO HAPPY TO BE ALIVE."

It's wild for me to reread those entries. In the beginning of the retreat, I was hungry, in pain, and tired … and yet both retreats end in sentiments of the purest joy simply to be alive. These entries were written a year apart, and yet they feel so similar. After ten days of speaking to no one, of no drinks, no electronics, no Internet, no food after twelve, and no friends – just me and my connection to spirit and the universe – I felt *so alive*. I experienced levels of gratitude and joy in a way I hadn't known before.

And it's going to feel similar for you as you begin to take the small steps each day implementing mindfulness into your daily life. At first, it might feel difficult, or frustrating, or maybe even annoying. And that's perfectly okay. The more you practice, and the more it becomes a regular part of your daily routine, you'll be able to shift into the joy, peace, focus, clarity, and creativity that comes with a regular practice – without having to spend ten days in silence.

Everything I achieved in those retreats is achievable with daily practice in simple, short exercises. In my Live Your Dreams program, we do simple exercises that take just five minutes a day, and the transformations are

At first, it might feel difficult, or frustrating, or maybe even annoying. And that's perfectly okay.

astounding when they're practiced consistently. Which is why I encourage everyone to make your practice a non-negotiable in your daily life. Just like eating dinner or brushing your teeth, making mindfulness practice a part of your daily routine has the potential to help you in ways you might not be able to imagine right now. Just trust me on that, if you can.

We are so often caught up in our life situation and the inner ramblings of the mind that it's like a cloudy day blocking out the sun of joy, clarity, and peace of mind within us. When we can practice quieting the mind, detaching from our thoughts, and simply letting things be, the cloudiness disappears, and the true beauty of life can present itself to you.

So I ask you, are you up for the challenge?

Will you choose discomfort if it means positive growth?

Or will you choose to remain in the discomfort you already know, and never move forward to the way of life that up until now, you've only been *wishing* you could live?

The Theories Behind Chapter 8

Have you ever driven home from somewhere and realize as you're pulling into the driveway that you have no idea which roads you took to get yourself there?

Or have you ever taken a shower, and as you turn off the water you can't remember if you actually shampooed your hair or not?

This is a sign that your brain is working overtime – and when we ask it to work overtime too often, it starts to break down.

We can't expect a triathlete to run a full triathlon every single day, can we? It's basic biology – that type of physical exertion on a daily basis would be detrimental to the body, and eventually it would give out.

And yet, we expect our brain to do work at its highest level each and every day without giving it the breaks and rest that it needs to function optimally. Your brain is an electrical circuit board that sends signals to the rest of your body so that it can function the way it does.

And for just a moment, imagine using a computer that has a virus. You're trying to send an email, but new windows are opening when you didn't ask them to. You try to close down a program, but it won't let you. All you want to do is just finish sending that email. And just when you think you're about to accomplish that task, the computer opens up five more tabs and you lose your place. Music is playing somewhere (you have no idea where) and you finally just unplug the damn thing and walk away frustrated.

And now understand that those tabs, the music, and those pop-up windows in the infected computer are just like your thoughts of fear, insecurity, self-doubt, worry, overthinking, and confusion that play out in your mind and continue to keep you from getting where you want to be in life.

It's like sitting at your desk at the office and your boss and coworkers just keep dropping off more and more paper and files onto your desk. You barely have a chance to open the first file – let alone work on it – when three more are dumped on top. You're trying to catch up to the workload, but it all just seems so overwhelming. You stay late every night, but the piles of folders don't seem to go down even an inch. Your body aches from sitting at the desk all day, and you know that any of the work you actually got done is full of typos and small errors because you just can't seem to focus anymore.

Just like you and I, or the triathlete I mentioned earlier, your brain needs rest and exercise to perform at its highest abilities.

And that's exactly what we can do with mindfulness practices and meditation.

When we give it the care it deserves and desires, we will see that the brain starts working *for us* instead of against us.

Meditation vs. Mindfulness

> *"Mindfulness is the awareness that emerges through paying attention on purpose, in the present moment, and non-judgmentally to the unfolding of experience moment by moment."*

> —Jon Kabat-Zinn

Jon Kabat-Zinn wins in my world for the best definition of mindfulness. I also like to explain it as being aware in the present moment and watching any thoughts or reactions that arise – rather than getting attached to or judging them. It's an awareness of our external reality and *how we are reacting to it* – instead of simply reacting to it on autopilot. The more hours of our day that we can live in this state, the less we will find ourselves getting angry, frustrated, sad, or stressed – because those emotions arise from thought, and when we can watch the thought before we attach to it or become consumed by it, we can choose our response instead of simply reacting.

For those who find themselves unsure of which roads they took to get home, they are far from present in the moment. They are far from a mindful state.

If mindfulness is a state of being, mindfulness meditation is the exercise we do to get there.

It's comparable to going to the gym. If it's 6-pack abs we're looking for, then the meditation is the crunches and exercises you do to get there.

But it doesn't have to be on a cushion. These practices can be done anywhere at any time, by simply becoming fully present with your immediate surroundings.

Mindfulness helps you get out of your own damn way!

As we've discussed in depth, the only thing keeping us from achieving what we truly want in life is our own thoughts. Our own fears, worries, anxieties, doubts, etc.

And the more we practice mindfulness and meditation, the larger the gap – or the pause – becomes between something happening in our life and our response to it. We increase our ability to watch our thoughts rather than be consumed by them.

Just because we think something, doesn't make it true. Can you think of a time when you were excited about doing something in life? Perhaps you spent an afternoon or some significant chunk of time thinking about how amazing it would be if you did x, y, or z. Then all of a sudden, you get a waft of thoughts that bring you back to 'reality'. You start thinking about how difficult that would actually be, and you have bills to pay, and this, that, and the other … and so perhaps you actually can't or shouldn't do it. It's irresponsible. And your excitement turns quickly to defeat, maybe even sadness.

Or perhaps you start getting excited about a new romantic relationship. You're so excited about this person and how you feel when you're around them. And then all of a sudden you're hit with these thoughts of 'What if they change their mind? What if they cheat on me? What if they don't like me as much as I like them? What if they don't want the same things?' and instantly the joy and excitement you felt is replaced with fear, worry, and anxiety.

Or you're interviewing for a new job. You're so excited about the possibilities that this job could create for you in the future, and you start to daydream about coming home and telling your friends and family that you got the job! They're so proud of you, and quite frankly you're proud of yourself! And then *boom* … a waft of thoughts come in, 'Maybe I'm not actually qualified enough! I wonder who I'm up against, and if they're more qualified than me. What if I freeze in the interview and they think I'm an idiot?" and so your excitement for that job quickly turns into anxiety and self-doubt. Maybe you even debate cancelling the interview. What's the point, right?

In these situations, we too often allow the follow-up thoughts to deplete our mood and positive energy. We *were* excited, but then the 'reality' of the situation wafted in and changed our state of being.

But here's the thing … Neither one is any more true than the other.

All of it is thought.

All of it is thought that *we* created for ourselves.

We think we have found an amazing romantic partner (THAT'S A THOUGHT). We wonder if they'll cheat on us (ANOTHER THOUGHT). We're excited about a new potential job and what that could do for us (THOUGHT). We wonder if we're actually good enough to get it (THOUGHT). We have a wonderful new idea that feels exciting and would create joy in our life (THOUGHT). We don't think we *should* do it - it's not responsible (THOUGHT).

Everything that happens in our mind is simply a thought created by our own imagination. We imagine the good, and we imagine the bad. The issue that comes up for most people is that our brain gets stuck on the bad. In an effort to keep us safe, it starts to imagine all the ways a situation could go wrong, and it focuses on the potential 'danger' it perceives in the situation. However, 99.9% of the time, there is no inherent danger. It's simply fear about something that may or may not happen in the future.

And so you can choose to change your thoughts.

Choose the Thoughts that Serve You Best

Where our attention goes, our energy flows.

When we put our attention on the negative thoughts that we imagine, our energy moves toward those. And *boom*, we begin to see evidence of that.

So when we walk into an interview with an attitude and energy of 'I'm not qualified for this position', guess what's going to happen? They're also going to think you're not qualified, and you're not going to get the job!

When you engage in a romantic relationship and all you think about is how they might leave you or cheat on you, so you become jealous, demanding, needy, which results in high chances that they'll end up leaving you or cheating on you, because they don't feel they have a good relationship.

When you focus on the possible difficulties you *might* come across if you attempt to follow your dreams, then guess what – all you're going to see are difficulties and reasons why you shouldn't continue.

Now, if you decide to follow your dreams and create a life you've been dreaming of and focus your attention on the fact that while there may be challenges along the way, you're committed and excited to achieve the results, then guess what – you'll find it exciting and much easier than if you focus on the difficulties.

And the more we practice quieting the mind with meditation and mindfulness practices, the more opportunity we have to watch these thoughts arise and *choose* which ones we will focus on. We get to *choose* the thoughts that will move us in the direction of where we want to be in life, instead of the thoughts that will lead us away from that life.

I've been practicing mindfulness for almost a decade now, and I still have those fears, worries, and doubts pop up – but the difference is that I can see them now for what they are – just random thoughts – and I can choose not to get attached to them. I can choose to replace the negative thoughts with positive ones instead.

I often find myself saying, "Well that's not a helpful thought is it, Kandis?" and I laugh to myself out loud or in my mind, and I flip the thought around. For example, even writing this book I noticed a thought I was telling myself, 'What if it sucks, and people laugh at me for it?' and as I heard it in my mind, my eyes popped out, and I responded, 'Yeah, that would suck. But I'll never know whether it's awesome or terrible unless I finish writing the damn thing.' And so I finished the book as you can see here.

Practicing mindfulness and meditation won't completely stop those nasty little thoughts from popping up, because we're human. We have thoughts. But a regular practice *will* help you to see those thoughts as nothing more than thoughts that you can choose to believe and attach to, or not.

Take Your Thoughts to Court

Just because we think it, doesn't make it true.

Just because we think it, doesn't make it true.

Just because we think it, doesn't make it true.

Got it?

Just because we think it, doesn't make it true.

As you already now know, we have up to 60,000 thoughts per day. And if I had to guess, I'd say that 95% of those are complete bullshit thoughts. What if this ... What if that ... I should have done ... I could have done ... I would have done ... It would be terrible if ... etc., etc., etc.

The majority of our waking life we experience thoughts of completely useless crap. And as we know, most of it is negative.

I invite you to notice your thoughts for the next few days, and CHALLENGE THEM! Take them to court! Are these thoughts facts? Or just stories? Is it helpful in any way to continue thinking about them? Or would it be more beneficial to ask them kindly to leave?

When you realize that all your thoughts (other than things like 'I have to pee') are stories – you can then *choose* to create stories that are more helpful! Realize they're stories you're telling yourself, and then choose to think and believe something else instead!

Begin to take notice of what negative things you are thinking about. Are you being mean to yourself? Are you worrying about things that you can't actually do anything about in the moment? Are you thinking about things in the past that you wish you could change but you can't?

Notice them.

Write them down.

Then flip them around.

For example, 'The rent is due on the 30th, and I really wish I made more money so things would be easier.'

When you notice a thought such as that, ask yourself, 'Is there anything I can do to make more money and/or make things easier?'

If the answer is yes, go do that. If the answer is no, accept it as your current reality.

In reply to that thought you could say, 'Yeah, more money would be great, but at least I have a roof over my head for which I'm grateful.'

Alternatively, make a plan to find a way to create more money in your life!

But regardless, quit thinking about the fact that you 'wish' you had more money. Either find a way to get more money, or stop thinking about it, and be grateful for what you do have.

And at first, this is going to feel difficult. Your mind is going to fight you on your positive reframe. It wants to continue to think about these negative things, but we both know it's actually not helpful. And so stay strong, and continue to think those positive thoughts.

And practice even just FIVE minutes of meditation per day.[6]

Meditation Changes Your Brain

Neurons that fire together, wire together.

When we consistently practice meditation and shifting our thoughts from negative to positive, we basically create new habits in the thinking brain. The more we choose to create positive thoughts and invite negative thoughts to leave, the more we strengthen the neural pathways that create the positive thoughts. And over time, you'll feel fear, anxiety, worry, self-doubt, shame, and sadness less and less.

The following meditation demonstrates this in more depth. If you'd like to listen to the guided version, go to www.kandisjames.com/neuroplasticity

Otherwise, I'll invite you to read the following in a relaxed state and close your eyes when you're done to really allow the message to sink in and see what learnings come up for you.

---

6   For a complete library of guided meditations and instructional videos to start your journey into mindfulness meditation go to: www.kandisjames.com/meditationbundle

Neuroplasticity Meditation

I want you to imagine that you're driving a pretty large vehicle that doesn't have the best handling. It's definitely not a 4-wheel drive. And you come to a fork in the road. One road goes through a forest. There are some tree branches covering bits of the road. You can see a few boulders on the path, a few potholes. It doesn't look easy. And the other road ... well it is clear and smooth – you can see ahead of you for days. You'd likely choose the clear road, right?

But now what if I tell you that at the end of the covered, more difficult road is a gorgeous blue/green lake at the bottom of an immense mountain range. There are fruit trees and raspberry bushes everywhere. Animals are playing, birds are chirping. And at the end of the clear road there's but a patch of dried up land, a bit of muddy water pooled in the middle with dead bugs floating in it. Not a tree in sight for shade, and no water for refreshment.

Now that you know the destination ... which road would you choose?

And so of course you want to take the road that takes you to the beautiful lake with the animals and fruit trees. You take it slowly at first, stopping to trim the trees in your way, perhaps move a boulder off the road. Your tire briefly gets stuck in a pothole, but you manage to get it out and keep moving. Eventually you get to the lake and you sit by that crystal blue lake, looking up at the mountain, taking in the view. But it took you a long time to get there, and so you don't stay long before heading back.

Then a few days later, you decide to go back to that lake, bringing a nice picnic lunch. You leave earlier this time so you can spend more time at the lake, but this time the road seems a bit easier. The trees were trimmed back just a few days ago, and you know where that pothole was that you got stuck in, so you manage to go around it. You get to that lake, and you sit there for a while with your picnic lunch, enjoying the sights ... the warm sun beating down on you and the gentle breeze brushing past. The birds chirping and the sound of water gently crashing into the lake's shore nearby.

And from there on out, each time you decide to go to the lake, to take that path, it gets a little bit easier, and you get to stay there just a little bit longer. Each time you go, it is faster and easier, as your tires make grooves on that road for you to follow. They wear down a path, and eventually you don't even remember why you considered going any other way.

Through neuroplasticity we can literally rewire our brain. Just like we can create a path to this beautiful lake in nature, we can create a path within our mind that brings us to peace. To calm. To a better way of living, of being, of engaging with ourselves and with others. Instead of trimming trees, we use meditation to light up positive neural pathways. And the more often we do this, the easier the path becomes to follow.

And so take a few moments to sit in silence and reflect on what you now know. How does it make you feel? How will this affect your practice? What will you do, based on what you now know? Now close your eyes and sit with this for a few moments, allowing what you've learned to sink in.

CHAPTER 9

Becoming the Creator of Your Life

THE TITLE OF this book is called *Get Outta Your Head and into your life.*

And so far, we've done a lot of talking about what it means to get out of your head. To recognize and challenge unhelpful thoughts, and to quiet the mind to tap into your intuition and guidance from the universe.

But what does that have to do with creating and living the life that you dream of?

Well... EVERYTHING.

You and those thoughts of yours are the only things getting in your way of living your best life

It's the fear, the limiting beliefs, and the negative thoughts on loop all day in your mind that are keeping you from achieving and accessing everything you want in this life.

When I look back at the version of who I was when I went on that date with a stranger whose name I don't remember – I barely recognize myself. I was so full of excuses as to why I couldn't do what I wanted in life. In fact, at that time I wasn't even really sure what it was I wanted to do; all I knew was that I wasn't doing it.

My time abroad helped me realize a lot of things. It helped me shed my skin, let go of what wasn't serving me, and learn new ways of being. Almost ten full years later I'm at last pursuing all of my business dreams, I'm finishing this book, and I'm loving who I've become and the direction in which I'm headed.

And I've also realized that this journey didn't need to take an entire decade.

I'm not saying it wasn't fun, because it most definitely was! And would I do it again? Heck yes. But what I realize now is that I could have had my incredible experience abroad *and* been accomplishing more goals along the way if I'd known the exact exercises, methods, and techniques that would help a little earlier. Which is good news for you, because if you're looking to change your life and create new possibilities for yourself but you're not able or ready to go on a solo trip abroad for seven years – don't worry!

This is exactly why I wrote this book, and it's exactly why I developed my *Live Your Dreams* program. And more good news – just by reading this book your own transformation has already begun.

See, one of the biggest realizations I've had since I've returned back home to Canada, is that the *greatest, most profound* transformations I experienced happened while I was simply sitting still and looking inward. The moments I chose to sit in silence and meditate – simply watching and listening to what was going on inside of me – those are some of the most powerful moments of change and transformation.

When I learned to quiet my overthinking mind and quit taking everything that popped into my head so gosh darn seriously – that's when I gained the most clarity. That's when I gained the confidence to move in the direction of my dreams.

Since then, I've actually created a nine-week program to show others how to do exactly what I've done for myself, in just a few short weeks instead of an entire decade.

And let me tell you – watching people inside my signature *Live Your Dreams (LYD)* program go from feeling lost, stuck, and unsure of what the future has in store for them to feeling empowered, positive, and excited about the future – it makes me feel *all* the good feels. Because what I learned out there in my travels and experience is now not only responsible for changing *my* life for the better, it's also responsible for changing many other lives for the better too! From my own experience, I've created a replicable system for you or anyone who wants to finally live their dreams!

Steps to Creating Your Dream Life

1. Choose to become the Creator

My LYD clients know how much I love to look at life as a game. I don't like life to be too serious. Why does it have to be so serious all the time? Why do so many people see everything as the be-all-end-all? Instead, we can learn to live life as though it's a fun game. And like any good game, we have the option to choose our playing piece – but we only have two choices in the game of life: The Victim or The Creator.

When we choose to become The Creator, we don't let life happen *to us,* but rather we create the life in front of us. The Creator knows that there is a *choice* in life, no matter what cards they are dealt in the beginning. And The Creator accepts the cards they've been dealt in this game called life and does the best with what they've got – staying positive, choosing actions and behaviors that will get them *closer to* their goals instead of further away from them. And The Creator plays to win – whatever that looks like to them.

2.   **Get clarity on what you want to do next in your life**

Once you choose to become the Creator of your own life, you've got to gain clarity on the direction in which you're moving. If you don't know your destination, how will you go the right way?

In this step, it's important to gain clarity on what it is that you *truly* want at the highest level. For example, I've had clients say to me, 'I want to start a business.' and I'll respond with 'For what reason?' They might say, 'To make money,' and I'll say, 'And what will that money give you?' We go on like this until we reach something high level such as 'freedom to spend lots of time with my kids and not worry about money.'

Many of my LYD clients have come into the program thinking that they want one thing in life, but it turns out as we go through these clarifying exercises that what they truly want is something completely different.

And the further we can dig into what it is you truly want

and why, the more opportunities you'll have to receive it. Remember that the universe doesn't always play a straight-forward game. So the more options we leave open to get to our final desired feeling, the more likely we'll reach it.

During this step it's of utmost importance to break free of what you believe you 'should do', and lean 100% into what your heart wants you to do. When we live from the heart, and from the body, we receive everything we need to create true happiness within.

3. Create a roadmap that will get you there

This is one of my favorite parts of the process. Once you have clarity on where you really want to go and what you truly want to achieve in the next chapter of your life, you've got to create your roadmap!

What will it take to get you from point A to point B?

You've got to get as specific as possible here. Specific, specific, specific.

And then get more specific.

When my LYD clients bring me their first draft of their roadmap, it is always far too vague, and far too complicated.

Don't choose 25 things to change about your life next week. Choose a maximum of three at a time, and then break those down.

Be specific.

And be prepared to get overwhelmed. Each time I've run the LYD program, the week of the roadmap knocks the wind out of people. So much so that we have an integration week that follows. So be gentle with yourself.

4. Remove the roadblocks and GO!

The roadblocks are a lot of what we've been talking about in this book. They're those nagging thoughts that are keeping you stuck in inaction and paralyzed in fear instead of getting you out there living your best damn life!

It's about noticing the way you feel – noticing the fear and self-doubt – and then flipping the script and getting out there and doing it anyway! It's go time!

Each week, each day, each moment, you've got to set your goals, and move forward in the direction of your dreams.

"But what if I don't know what my life purpose is?"

The Dalai Lama was once asked, "What is the meaning of life?"

To which he responded, "The meaning of life is happiness."

I see it frequently – both with my LYD clients and just out there in the world – this idea that we are meant to have this grand purpose in life, to have that one thing we've wanted to achieve our entire lives. And some people have that – some people see something they want at the age of ten, and they live their lives for it. But that's actually not the norm. At least, it sure wasn't for me, and most of my clients!

"Success" is an interesting word in our society

Many of us believe that success means lots of money, lots of travel, nice clothes, and the latest tech gadgets – am I right?

But what if success is simpler than that? What if success is simply the ability to be happy each and every day? To be able to be happy in a way that doesn't rely on anything in the external world – such as a romantic partner, a specific job, a career, a car, a house, a friend, family, or even a dog? What if true success meant doing what feels right in your heart? And the ability to cultivate happiness from within, wherever you are?

But that will never exist if we are constantly living within the worry of our mind. It will never exist if we are constantly in a negative thought loop or continue to resist what is. It will never exist if we don't step into the role of being The Creator of our life in each and every moment. And it will never exist if we live a life we think we *should* live, instead of living a life we deeply *want* to live.

What if success truly meant simply being happy?

And what if we realized that each one of us finds happiness in completely different ways?

I had a friend say to me recently amidst a deep conversation, "Well aren't we all looking for happiness somewhere? It's not realistic to be happy all the time."

And I beg to differ. I'm not looking for happiness anywhere. I simply *am* happy. Of course, certain situations will make me feel sad, angry, or frustrated, but the happiness never leaves. It is the core of my being, and no matter what goes on, I know that I can count on it being there. Because being alive and helping others in any way I can is what I need to be happy.

There is no life purpose, there's just what makes you happy

This is what I tell my students. Your success is unique to you. Your success is the ability to be happy as often as possible.

It's taken me a lot of practice to just 'be happy'. But it stemmed from letting go of the reins of what I perceived I 'should do', and doing what my heart, and my gut wanted me to do, instead of just listening to my head (or other people).

And that's what I want to see everyone else do too.

I had this dear friend who went through my *Live Your Dreams* program. She joined the program because her daughter was going to school soon, and the stay-at-home-mom life wasn't necessary anymore. She felt she should contribute to the family in a different way and get a job! Move forth in her career!

And when we got to the part of the program where we gained clarity and created that roadmap, what became incredibly clear is that a career didn't matter to her – what actually mattered was having a happy, healthy family who got to spend lots of time together and do the things they loved. She came into the program thinking she wanted to decide on a career or business venture, and within five weeks her and husband sold their house and moved across the country – something they'd been dreaming of doing for years but had been too scared to actually take action.

And that's what happens to most of us, right? We have dreams, but they seem too scary to implement. We get too caught up in all the possible negative outcomes, creating stories of the worst case scenarios, and wondering what other people will think of us – and so we freeze. We don't actually take action.

But like I said earlier – the only thing that's actually holding you back are your own thoughts and your own fears. Either you don't actually want it that much, or you're simply too scared to take the next step.

So what's holding you back now?

You know now that your own thoughts are the only things getting in the way of what you desire. And so what's holding you back?

What's keeping you from telling that person how you really feel?

What's keeping you from doing that thing you've wanted to do for so long?

What's keeping you from loving yourself instead of putting yourself down all the time?

What's keeping you from living the life of your dreams instead of dreaming about it?

Look deep inside of yourself. Are the reasons you came up with actually valid? Or are they simply an excuse?

Going after what your heart wants and going after your dreams isn't always *easy*. But it's worth it.

Over the years, when people learn about the adventures I've had and the places I've lived, I often hear that same thing I used to say … "I wish I could do that."

And then they'll tell me why they can't – they have kids, they have a spouse, they have a job, they have bills, they have parents, etc. But newsflash – we all have at least some of those.

There was a couple I met who rented the house beside my friend Asia in Chiang Mai. They were school teachers from Ireland. They were in their early thirties, and sitting at home in Ireland one day, they were chatting about how they wished they'd been able to travel before having kids. And then it struck them – they still could! So they sold their house, quit their jobs, packed up their kids, and moved to Thailand!

They'd been there for a year and a half by the time I left, and as far I know they're still there. They ended up getting great jobs in Chiang

Mai, and during their holidays from work they take their kids to the Philippines, Malaysia, Australia, and so many other places.

The point is ... if you truly want something, you can make it work if you're willing to.

There might be times of difficulty, as there is in any life you choose – but you have to ask yourself what you want the most.

When I travelled to Thailand and decided to stay, I gave up a lot of stuff from back home. I missed big family gatherings, weddings, and holidays. I missed special birthdays and fun outings. I made a much smaller salary in Thailand than I would in Canada, which meant I couldn't fly home often. But to me, the experience I was having was more important at the time. I needed the freedom to find myself.

There will always be a holiday, an event, or a special occasion that you can use as an excuse to keep you from doing what you truly want in this life. You can always say you don't have enough money, or you have too many responsibilities. You might tell yourself that you'll do it 'one day' or 'someday' but most people get to the end of their life and have never seen someday or one day.

I'm telling you ... no time will ever feel like 'the perfect time'. It's simply a choice you need to make.

So I ask you ... what is truly holding you back?

Notice Your Internal Narrative

Our thoughts create our reality.

So if you're not living the life you want in any way, notice where your thoughts are.

What we put our attention on, we receive.

If you continue to think about how much Bobby irritates you, Bobby is going to continue to irritate you!

If you continue to think of all the people who have wronged you in your life, you're going to see that more and more people wrong you in your lifetime.

If you continue to think of how little money you have and what a hard life you lead, you're only going to see it get worse.

If you continue to think of your anxiety – your anxiety is going to persist!

A simple shift in our thoughts can create incredible differences in our external reality.

As Dr. Shauna Shapiro recommends, start each day by asking yourself: *"What wonderful things will happen today?"*

And notice how your life begins to change for the positive as you shift your focus to the wonders of each day.

Your thoughts are powerful. *You* are powerful. What will you choose to do with that power?

Will you choose to be the victim of your life? Or will you choose to be the creator?

And if you choose to be the creator, what actions are you going to start taking *today* that will lead you towards your best life?

Want to take your learning further?

There are many ways you can continue to work with, connect, and learn from Kandis::

Social Media:

 @KandisJames.KJ

Podcast:

www.kandisjames.com/podcast

Live Your Dreams (LYD)

Kandis's signature program, *Live Your Dreams*, is an online group coaching program designed to help others just like you create a life they love to live each and every day.

www.kandisjames.com/liveyourdreams

What past students have said about *Live Your Dreams:*

 *"Live Your Dreams changed my life. I was stuck and this program unstuck me. It made me look in the mirror and tell the girl looking back that life is short, so take responsibility and stop being a victim to my circumstances. I can truly say I am now living my dream in reality. And I'm not finished. This program is something you take with you every day of your life. The skills are priceless. Thank you Kandis James for helping me transform my life. Thank you feel grateful to have been part of this program."*

—Reet German, Mother, Wife, and Adventurous Soul

"My life seems to be falling into place, things are happening. Things are moving along, and I'm not staying stagnant, and in that black hole that I felt I was in for such a long time."

—Candice, South Africa

"At the start of the Live Your Dreams program I identified myself as a wife, mother and counsellor. However, since doing the program I know that I am so much more. I have connected deeply to my own spirituality and see myself as a mentor, guide, and leader to other women. I am also clear that I am doing this for the women before me and the women still to come, which gives me my "why" and keeps me committed and focused. On the days when I doubt myself, I have so many powerful resources to "get out of my head and step into my life." It really is a life-changing program, and I feel incredibly blessed to have the experience to work with Kandis!"

—Janine Dowdell, Founder of A Woman's Way

"I'm excited again. I feel like I'm myself again, and I'm very positive and optimistic again. That's something that was kind of left behind and now I feel like I have it again in my life."

—Brenda, Peru

"I feel like anything is possible in this world … Whatever you dream, you can make it happen. And it doesn't have to take six years to make it happen either. It can happen in just eight weeks."

—Reet, Canada

Everyone – and I mean everyone – has a different idea of what success looks like in this life. Everyone has different ideas of what it means to create their dream life. Unfortunately, many people also believe that living their 'dream life' is nothing more than a fantasy. Inside *Live Your Dreams* we'll take the content of this book even further, you'll learn the exact methods and tools (like the roadmap!) that I used to create my own dream life, and that my students have used to:

- Travel the world
- Start a podcast
- Move across the country
- Give up their fear of starting a business
- Understand and get connected with their true purpose in this life
- Have a better relationship with their family/children
- Increase self-love and confidence
- Wake up feeling joyful and ready to conquer the world

So let me ask you … what are YOU waiting for? What's preventing YOU from finally living the life you've been dreaming of?[7]

Inside *Live Your Dreams* you'll learn how to get out of your own way, so you can create a life you love waking up to each and every day.

kandisjames.com/liveyourdreams

---

7 Hint: the only thing holding you back is you!

SOME OF MY FAVORITE BOOKS:

A Fearless Heart – Thupten Jinpa, PhD
Aware – Dan Siegel, MD
Buddha's Bedroom – Cheryl Fraser, PhD
Dissolve the Problem – Richard Dotts
Freedom – Osho
Good Morning, I Love You – Shauna Shapiro, PhD
Joy on Demand – Chade-Meng Tan
Revolution – Russell Brand
Super Brain – Deepak Chopra, MD and Rudolph E. Tanzi, PhD
The Buddha's Brain – Rick Hanson, PhD
The Four Agreements – Don Miguel Ruiz
The Power of Now – Eckhart Tolle
The Tao of Pooh – Benjamin Hoff

Made in the USA
Monee, IL
07 July 2026

56551426R00142